FFESTINIOG ADVENTURE

ADVENTURE

The Festiniog Railway's Deviation Project

DAVID & CHARLES

Newton Abbot London North Pomfret (VT)

British Library Cataloguing in Publication Data
Hollingsworth, John Brian
Ffestiniog adventure.
1. Festiniog Railway
2. Railroads – Wales – Ffestiniog region –
Conservation
I. Title
385'.5'0942929   HE3821.F44
ISBN 0-7153-7956-9

© Brian Hollingsworth 1981

Set by Latimer Trend & Company Ltd, Plymouth
and printed in Great Britain by
Redwood Burn Ltd, Trowbridge, Wilts.
for David & Charles (Publishers) Limited
Brunel House Newton Abbot Devon

Published in the United States of America
by David & Charles Inc
North Pomfret Vermont 05053 USA

Contents

3

Foreword

As Chairman of the Festiniog Railway Company, I must publicly state that we owe a great debt of gratitude to so many people.

The Festiniog Railway Society of course comes first because without their effort there would not have been any Festiniog Railway after 1954. Ever since then, complete restoration to Blaenau Ffestiniog has always been the main objective of both Company and Society. Even so, the fact that this is now in sight simply would not have been possible without the quite fantastic volunteer civil engineering project known as the Deviation.

One day, perhaps about 1982, the first train for over 40 years will enter the centre of Blaenau Ffestiniog preceded probably by a silver band and with great festivity and celebration. No doubt credit will be given to the Company, the Society and the various Government agencies who will have channelled nearly £2 million in capital aid towards the project, as well as the local authorities who have all helped so greatly.

When in this way Blaenau Ffestiniog becomes a flourishing tourist centre because of its rail links to north and south, it is hoped that this book will enable people to appreciate the efforts of these invaders of the mountains from Britain and beyond. In any case it is a record of the debt the Company, as well as the communities the railway benefits, owe to the Deviationists for making the restoration possible.

JOHN ROUTLY

Preface

The Deviationists: 'we don't want a whitewash job, write about us as you find us'. Gerard Fiennes: 'Remember it was all done for fun'. Francis Wayne: 'Promise me you'll get the Chairman's approval for anything you say'. Bunny Lewis: 'Put it all in, nausea and everything'. Richard Lemon: 'Don't forget Liza the one-eyed sheep'.

With these and a multitude of similar contradictory admonitions ringing in my ears, I set out on the notoriously perilous task of recording recent history, with this book the result. My grateful thanks are due to all those lovers of the Festiniog Railway who gave their help, either by coming long distances to recount their experience or supplying Deviation documentation by the box full.

And for all those who worked on or for the project, my undying admiration for what they did and how they did it. I have tried also to record the Deviationists' gratitude due to the many organisations and individuals who presented (knowingly or unknowingly!) goods or services to aid the Cause. Hopefully, no conscious benefactor has been forgotten; if so, it was certainly not deliberate.

My thanks are also due to those who allowed their photographs and drawings to be reproduced; also for permission to reprint a number of extracts from the *Festiniog Railway Magazine*. I also owe a great deal to Messrs John Routly, Michael Schumann, Chris Chitty, Chris Noel, Bunny Lewis, David Yates and Allan Garraway who went through the manuscript and made valuable suggestions, while the debt of gratitude owed to Margot Cooper who typed it all out, is almost too great to go into words.

Penrhyndeudraeth, 1980   BRIAN HOLLINGSWORTH

I

Love for a railway

'The act of love was nothing like what she had
expected, and they did not reach any great summit
together . . . but she knew when it was done that
they had together set their feet on a great mountain'.
John Masters   Far, Far the Mountain Peak

One hundred years ago, several hundred miles of railway
were being built in Britain every year. Why, then, make a fuss
about a project which involved an average of a quarter-mile
annually? There is one main reason – that from Chairman of
the Festiniog Company down to a one-day-only volunteer, it
was done not to make money, to wage war, serve political ends
or to facilitate commerce (the usual reasons for building
railways) but for Love; or, in the case of some, for what is really
a similar reason, Fun. The letters JGF (standing, with sometimes just a hint of sarcasm, for 'Jolly Good Fun') make
inconspicuously conspicuous appearances around and about
the FR from time to time.

Railways in general all seem to inspire affection in mankind,
but the Festiniog is special – perhaps a brief look at its history
will be a part explanation. The Festiniog Railway Company
(with only one 'F', please note – see Appendix A) was incorporated by Act of Parliament in 1832, before Queen
Victoria came to the throne. It was promoted in order to build
a horse-, rope- and gravity-worked 2ft gauge tramway from
Blaenau Ffestiniog (two 'F's this time) in North Wales to the
sea at Porthmadog. The object was to provide transport for
slate mined in the area down to the port for shipment. The line
was so laid out that, apart from the negotiation of a certain ridge

9

in the mountains (about which there will be a great deal more later), the trains of slate trams could gravitate literally by gravity steadily down to the bottom. Horses pulled the empty wagons back up the hill to the quarries, having travelled down in special dandy cars, as they were known. The mountain ridge was crossed by two rope-worked inclines; the one which took the loaded wagons up-hill was powered by a water-wheel; the other, on which loaded wagons went down and empty ones up, needed nothing but a brake.

An improvement which was soon made involved the by-passing of the two inclines by boring the 750yd Moelwyn tunnel, completed in 1842, the existence and alignment of which is closely linked with the deviation project. Topo-graphically speaking, this ridge through which Moelwyn Tunnel is bored, presented the only major obstacle to locating the railway in an easy position on the side of a hill almost all the way down. Following the contours is particularly easy for a narrow gauge line, because of the sharp curves that such a line can negotiate. Full-size trains of 4ft 8½in or standard gauge, can pass at low speeds on curves as sharp as 500ft radius, whereas our 1ft 11⅝in gauge line has curves of 120ft radius. This makes it that much easier to go round obstacles rather than through them.

Some twenty years later, with trade booming, 52,000 tons of slate were carried annually and the capacity of the line was reached. Proposals were made for a separate conventional normal gauge railway, but Charles Spooner, the son of James Spooner who had engineered the original tramway, proposed the then revolutionary idea of converting the line, in spite of the absurdly small distance between the rails, to the first narrow-gauge steam public passenger railway in the world. It was a pioneer in many ways for among its motive power were some unique bogie 0–4–4–0T steam locomotives (the 'Fairlies') and it ran the first bogie (8-wheel) iron-framed passenger coaches in Britain from the early 1870s. The gauge of the line, which had been a rather nominal 2ft, was set at 600 millimetres or 1ft 11⅝in, for Spooner was an early metric enthusiast. The Festiniog Railway opened in its new guise in 1864, soon achieving world-wide renown and a good deal of imitation – the sincerest form of flattery – much of it ill-advised. Everyone was keen on the idea of building such a cheap form of railway, but they often under-estimated the extra costs and other handicaps involved in interchange with normal gauge railways. Festiniog slate traffic then rose to a peak, just before the turn of the century, of 139,000 tons a year.

The years rolled by, the slate trade declined and the motor bus took away local passengers; the Festiniog attempted to survive by offering tourists rides on a 'toy railway' (I quote from posters of the day) amongst some of the loveliest scenery in the world. It was very well situated for this trade, with connections at Blaenau Ffestiniog to the North Wales coast resorts and to Cardigan Bay places at its southern end, by standard gauge railways belonging to the London Midland & Scottish and Great Western companies respectively. Passenger traffic did not rise in overall terms but its decline from 164,000 in 1922 to 46,000 in 1939 was alleviated by such measures.

The second world war took away the tourists; in 1946 even the remaining vestigial slate movement came to an end and at once nature took over. The company had big debts and virtually no resources except some scrap metal and (almost) valueless land; because it was advised that parliamentary powers were required to abandon its undertaking, even these could not be realised. This stalemate was still (fortunately) in being eight years later, when a resourceful railway enthusiast called Alan Pegler, helped by the present company chairman John Routly and many others, managed to acquire a controlling interest in the Festiniog Company, with the idea of restoring and re-opening the line. It was a daunting task and they soon realised the size of the mountain upon which they had set their feet.

A token service was run across the great embankment ('The Cob') from Porthmadog to Boston Lodge during the peak

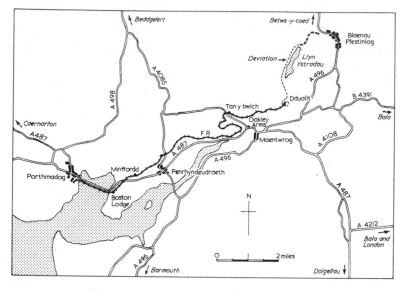

Fig 1   A general map of the Festiniog Railway

period of the 1955 season. Penrhyndeudraeth was reached in
1956 and Tan-y-Bwlch in 1958. Nearly all the work of
clearance, restoration and operation of services was done by
volunteers, that is, people who gave their services free because
they wanted to see the Festiniog Railway running again.
Indeed, in most cases, it cost the volunteers money to work,
since food, accommodation and transport to North Wales had
to be paid for out of their own pockets. They set themselves up
as the Festiniog Railway Society, in support of the FR
Company. As will be told, the Company Board naturally had
its eyes on the rails beyond Tan-y-Bwlch to Blaenau Ffestiniog
and its connection with north coast resorts; but it was to be ten
years before the by then more commercially-minded Festiniog
felt strong enough to re-open any more line.

You might think that there is some contradiction here with
what was said in the opening paragraph. In fact, there is none
because in the present day Festiniog context, 'commercially-

minded' refers more to the unfortunate need to think commercially in order to survive, than to a desire for profit in the
sense of clinking money-bags for the owners. In fact, the shares
of the Festiniog Railway are owned by a non-profit-making
registered Charitable Trust.

Although the railway did not run public services above
Tan-y-Bwlch until 1968, works trains found their way on
various occasions via Dduallt, Moelwyn Tunnel and Tan-y-
Grisiau through to Blaenau Ffestiniog. The objective was
usually the recovery of serviceable track material, but one
notable exception was a special train conveying FR
representatives to a meeting to discuss terms for the take-over
by the British Electricity Authority (as it then was – we now
know it as the Central Electricity Generating Board) of a
supposedly derelict section of the line, for a hydro-electric
scheme, quite a surprise for the electricity men! Even so, the
take-over, under compulsory powers, took place on 6 February
1956; hence the writing of this book.

On one of the trips through the tunnel to Blaenau Ffestiniog
with the aim of recovering some track materials, a conflict of
opinion arose over the ownership of some lineside scrap, quite
near the site of the present power station. One thing led to
another and eventually vocal conflict led to physical conflict
and the police had to be summoned. . . . but the aspect of the
affair that struck the minion of the law when he arrived was not
so much the fighting as the fact that it was going on on a
Sunday!

All this (and much more) is set out in two excellent books; a
definitive history called *The Festiniog Railway* in two volumes
by J. I. C. Boyd (Oakwood Press, 1975), and a more personal
account *The Little Wonder* by John Winton, published jointly
by the Festiniog Railway Company and Michael Joseph,
during 1977.

2

Hydro-electric harassment

'Power tends to corrupt and absolute power corrupts
absolutely.'

Lord Acton   The Life of Mandell Creighton

If the civil engineering of the Festiniog Deviation was by
professional standards relatively trivial, the legal aspects of
it were not only big but the biggest. The recourse to the law in
order to obtain reasonable compensation from the Central
Electricity Generating Board for the compulsory acquisition
of a stretch of the FR's line of route, began in 1956 and reached
a settlement in 1972. The 16½-year case was the longest in
British legal history, the nearest rivals being the case of the
claimant to the Tichborne Estate, which took 13¼ years
(1871–84) and the 9-year trial of Warren Hastings (1786–95).

The trio of able men on the Board who guided the Company
through the labyrinth of little-known legal pathways and who
defended its point of view before umpteen legal and other
courts from the House of Lords downwards, must be saluted at
its happy conclusion: John Routly, solicitor by training,
industrialist by profession, Vice-Chairman until 1972 and
subsequently Chairman; Francis Wayne, Secretary to the
Festiniog and numerous other companies, Director until 1971;
and Leslie Smith, by profession a surveyor, still serving on the
Festiniog Railway Board as Deputy Chairman.

One must also say that, were there such things as Guardian
Angels for railways, the Festiniog's was certainly on duty during
the quarter-century covered by this narrative. She was
definitely there around 1952 making certain the old FR Board
never grasped the fact that the British Electricity Authority's

Bill was an opportunity to have written in to it authority to abandon their railway and so realise its meagre assets. One might also add to her credit the fact that the new Board arrived when it did in the nick of time and contained such a plethora of legal and actuarial acumen. If the take-over had happened a year or two earlier the deviation could have easily been written into the North Wales Hydro-Electric Power Act (or, just as easily, the scheme could have been re-located), but then the opportunity for the wonderful goings-on described in this book would never have arisen; a year or two later and the opportunity would have passed for ever.

Someone's hand was also guided so that when compensation finally did come in 1972, it was spent at once instead of lying languishing in the bank waiting for contracts to be let and so losing its value during the vicious inflation then about to happen. It seems also almost more than a coincidence that successive waves of taxpayers' money (the Wales Tourist Board, the Development Board for Rural Wales and the Manpower Services Commission) were available just as they were wanted, together with a Chairman whose drive and familiarity with the Corridors of Power so often turned these flows of largesse in the Festiniog's rather than in anyone else's direction.

The Devil, of course, was also present; He certainly planted hatred in the minds of both sides. The Electricity Board had the conviction that Alan Pegler and Co, had bought up a moribund railway cheap entirely with a view to extracting from them for personal gain a five-figure sum; hence the Board saw themselves riding white chargers into battle to save taxpayers' money placed in their care from falling into the hands of the Infidel. The FR Board, on the other hand, felt themselves in the position of good little David facing Goliath. In fact, both sides had the purest of motives, so much so, in fact, that neither of them believed the other for a long, long time; indeed this is a sad commentary on the normal ways of the world.

Incidentally, this was no fancy speculation, but sober truth;

Alan Pegler and John Routly found this out rather abruptly while waiting to meet their opposite numbers at the British Electricity Authority's headquarters. To while away a rather long wait they idly thumbed through some papers left around (no doubt by carelessness rather than design) in the waiting-room; to their shocked amazement it was a briefing to Lord Citrine that they (Alan and John) were effectively a pair of pirates. When at last the meeting began, 30 BEA men were found to be present. At the FR's request, 28 were ejected, leaving the two Chairmen and two Vice-Chairmen alone. The question of motive was raised, upon which the FR men got up to go. In the end they were prevailed upon to stay and a useful exchange of views resulted, but the matter was not really set right for 17 years, when John Routly (then FR Chairman) was invited to a placatory lunch at CEGB HQ.

The old FR management had been informed late in 1951 of a proposal (subsequently abortive) for a conventional hydro-electric scheme, involving the same flooding of the line at Tan-y-Grisiau. They replied that there was no objection as the line was closed. When the scheme was revived a year or two later in its new guise as a pumped storage system, the new FR management only got to hear of it through overhearing conversations in the bar of the Oakley Arms Hotel at Maentwrog – the BEA's consulting engineers also quenched their thirsts in that famous hostelry!

Perhaps the injustice of the compensation law case has to a great extent been corrected by Government and Government Agency grants of taxpayers' money towards the material costs of the Deviation. An error of history has had to be put right, but at great cost to the country as a whole.

Francis Wayne spelt out the most devilish aspect of the whole affair in an article in the February/March 1972 issue of *Freedom First*, the Journal of The Society for Individual Freedom:

> If without malice or deliberate maladministration, and with the safeguard of a patient hearing by an independent tribunal, this

sort of thing can still happen, it is terrifying to think what chance the citizen would have if there was any deliberate misuse of power. The case has disclosed a degree of injustice and of weakness in the law which cannot be ignored either by Parliament or by any citizen who cares for freedom and fair dealings between Government and Public. All electors who care about these things should write to their MP and demand a review of the law relating to compensation and the extension of the powers of the Ombudsman to public bodies so that, even if Parliament cannot control its own creations, it can at least obtain independent reports on their administration.

All this opportunity for legal high-jinks arose from the fact that electricity, once produced, cannot be stored for use later, a property which it shares with newspapers and ripe tomatoes. An indirect way of storing electricity, however, is to use it to pump water up to a lake near the top of a mountain; later, when it is needed, the water can be allowed to run back through the pumps, which are of the type that can also function as turbines. Then, when the whole nation suddenly switches on its electric kettles at the end of Coronation Street, say, a handy slug of power is available at instant notice. To make this possible you need one reservoir high up and one low down, situated as close together as can be. If the cost of doing all this is to be kept within reasonable bounds then the choice of site is fairly limited, for the topography has to meet precise requirements. One place where these requirements were met was south of Blaenau Ffestiniog, but at the site in question the proposed lower reservoir would engulf a stretch of the grass-grown derelict Festiniog Railway.

The first shots of the legal battle were fired early in 1955 when the FR vainly opposed the Bill during its final stages, when Alan Pegler appeared in front of a House of Lords select committee. It was 'five of them to one of me', he says. There was a lot of stuff about 'old gentlemen and boys playing trains' and inevitably the Bill received the Royal Assent on 16 May, 1955. Formal 'Notice to Treat' came on 5 February, 1956 and 'Notice to Enter' on the following day. A second 'Notice to

Treat' in respect of Moelwyn Tunnel was received on 2 June, 1958; this time two days were allowed before 'Notice to Enter' was given.

It was now a question of claiming compensation; the justice and amount of any claim was adjudicated by a body known as the Lands Tribunal. The Lands Tribunal was empowered to award compensation calculated under a variety of alternative headings. The one that the Festiniog Railway wanted was of course 'equivalent reinstatement', that is to say, that the CEGB (in which way the builders of the hydro-electric scheme will in future be referred to, although at this time they were then still called the British Electricity Authority), should pay the costs of building a deviation line.

After discussions with them, the FR Company asked an FR Society life member called Charles Goode to make a survey. A simple scheme running around the west side of the new lake-to-be and which could be incorporated in the designs for the new power station, was devised and agreed. The cost was estimated at £80,000, at normal contractors' prices. Such a sum, mere loose change today, was then astronomical by railway preservation standards – in 1958 the whole FR turn-over was but £9,051, while now it is over £500,000.

At about the same time, either by accident or design, but in any case without telling the FR, the CEGB altered the plans. By moving the site of a switching station, Charles Goode's scheme was made impractical. Now came the turn of con-sulting engineers Livesay & Henderson, who produced a scheme for a route running on the east side of the new lake at an estimated cost of £180,000, more than double that of the 'Goode' scheme. This ploy achieved results which were on the face of it beneficial to the CEGB, because of the complicated rules and precedents which governed whether or not an 'equivalent reinstatement' should be allowed. If the cost of doing so exceeded the value of the business (calculated in some esoteric legal way), then 'equivalent reinstatement' was considered too expensive. In May 1960, the President of the

Lands Tribunal ruled that 'equivalent reinstatement' at £180,000 would only now be justified if passenger journeys could be increased from 76,000 to 196,000 and this he did not consider to be 'within the bounds of the possible.' This in legal terms still ranks as a 'finding of fact' despite the fact that the 'impossible' traffic figure was passed in 1967! The Court of Appeal upheld the Lands Tribunal decision, but confirmed that compensation would be payable under the heading of 'severance and disturbance'. Effectively such a sum would be based on the loss of business profit during the period of disturbance.

The main problem was that business profits were one thing that the FR had precious little of, either then or now. A railway suffering from a 50-year period of neglect has an inexhaustible appetite for hard cash. Accordingly, a concept called 'deferred maintenance' was evolved, by which the 'profits', both with and without the connection to Blaenau Ffestiniog, were calculated on the fictional basis that the Company had taken over a railway in good condition.

For the purposes of the claim for 'loss of profits', then, current maintenance was charged before arriving at the figure for profit, but the cost of repairing past neglect was regarded as a capital expense and ignored when calculating profit. This basis was accepted by the Lands Tribunal. It should be noted that accounting for a statutory railway is different from most commercial business in that there is no such thing as 'depreciation', because a railway is assumed always to be kept in perfect condition. The balance sheet therefore shows the costs of replacement of all the assets as if they were in perfect condition; in the FR's case 'deferred maintenance' was shown as a deduction. This has now been overtaken and the balance sheet now shows assets of about £4,000,000!

Nothing has so far been said about the time-consuming effort put in by individual members of the FR Board during all these wrangles. Computed at normal professional rates it would have represented a very large sum indeed – but, being for the

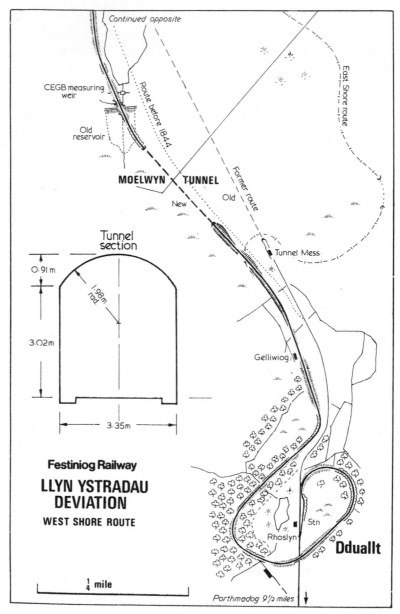

Continued opposite

CEGB measuring weir

Old reservoir

Route before 1844

East Shore route

MOELWYN TUNNEL

Former route

New

Old

Tunnel Mess

Tunnel section

0.91 m

1.98 m rad

3.02m

3.35m

Gelliwiog

Festiniog Railway

LLYN YSTRADAU DEVIATION

WEST SHORE ROUTE

Stn

Rhoslyn

Dduallt

¼ mile

Porthmadog 9½ miles

Fig 2   A detailed map of the deviation as built between Dduallt and Tan-y-Grisiau. *Dan Wilson*

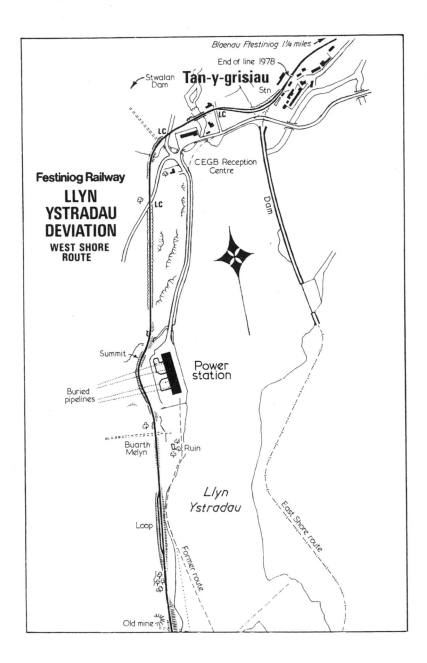

Blaenau Ffestiniog 1¼ miles

End of line 1978

Tan-y-grisiau

Stwalan
Dam

Stn

LC

LC

CEGB Reception
Centre

Festiniog Railway
LLYN
YSTRADAU
DEVIATION
WEST SHORE
ROUTE

LC

Dam

Summit

Power
station

Buried
pipelines

Buarth
Melyn

Ruin

*Llyn
Ystradau*

Loop

Former route

East Shore route

Old mine

Festiniog Railway, it was done at no charge. A particular result of the Board declaring their intentions so often before the highest courts in the land was that what had started off as 'a good idea if it could be managed' now became an iron resolve. In fact an iron resolve was needed, because the new basis for compensation meant that the Board would have to commit themselves to the huge cost of a deviation in the hope that the chancy course of litigation would, quite contrary to experience so far, in the end turn out to be in the FR's favour.

And so it did. Eventually, moreover, during the course of the final Lands Tribunal hearings and after a certain amount of behind-the-scenes pressure had been applied, the CEGB became friendly and allowed the cheaper route. Able engineers and hard-working labourers gave their services free, and various Government agencies fell over themselves to press folding money into the FR's hands. Because the Company had to wait, the explosion of traffic on the railway made the calculated loss of profits even better and, hence, on 11 October, 1972 the FR was awarded legal costs and £65,000 compensation, plus £30,000 interest. The *Festiniog Railway Magazine* declared 'It's a relief to be out of the metallic and uncertain hands of the law! In a court, as in a newspaper, familiar matters take on a certain unreality; for example, talking about deferred maintenance and a certain locomotive boiler. . . .

Witness for FR Co: 'The only justification for not charging that cost against profits is that the boiler should have been renewed many years ago, before 1962 . . .'

Counsel for CEGB: 'But the old boiler had been busy pulling trains on the Festiniog down to the time that it had burst . . .'

Witness: 'I did not think it had burst . . .'

The writer declares his unwillingness (and unfitness) to summarise the details of the Lands Tribunal case decision. One either accepts that the FR won a brilliantly and, incidentally, cordially fought legal battle and leaves it at that, or reads the whole of Mr H. P. Hobbs' clear but complex judgment. Those who wish to savour the details should accordingly turn to Appendix A, in which it is set out in full.

Finally, one should perhaps ask the question – was all this just for the sake of playing trains? The Festiniog's answer as set out by Francis Wayne in a document for the guidance of the lawyers who directed the case for the railway, was:

1. The original Constitution of the Company was to operate the whole line. This constitution can only be altered by Act of Parliament.

2. The Board of the FR were satisfied that the complete restoration of the line would be economically justified by estimates of the traffic to be expected.

3. The Festiniog (Railway) in the old days had always been part of the fastest route from London to Porthmadog, and a vital link in the railway system between North Wales and the Cambrian Coast. Recent events have made this aspect even more important with the closure of British Railways' lines from Caernarfon to Afon Wen and from Ruabon to Barmouth Junction, together with the down-grading of the line from Shrewsbury to Paddington.

3

Deviation alternatives

'I'm very well acquainted, too, with matters
mathematical I understand equations both the
simple and quadratical About binominal theorem
I'm teeming with a lot o' news With many cheerful
facts about the square of the hypotenuse.'
                    W. S. Gilbert   Pirates of Penzance

The writer must confess to a 50-year passion for choosing
railway routes – in fact, ever since he could connect two sections
of Hornby tinplate track together. Although since then there
have been adequate opportunities in various sizes from 'Dublo'
to 4ft 8½in he still greatly envies Gerald Fox's opportunity in
1962–1963 to choose one for the Festiniog.

An acceptable railway alignment has to satisfy strict
conditions as regards gradients and curvature, otherwise trains
of reasonable capacity cannot be worked at all and therefore
it is necessary to keep to these limits, even if the terrain is steep
and broken. However, one can often – literally – wriggle out
of problems by curving the line, so putting in a little extra
distance and hence, gaining a little extra height without
steepening the gradient. The same thing can be done by
zig-zagging back and forth; this has been done on various
mountain railways overseas but is almost unknown in Britain.

A third alternative is to change the rules, that is, to decide
that keeping to a gradient no steeper than elsewhere on the
line is too expensive and accordingly designing an alignment
with more severe grades. But reduced train loads or the need
for more powerful locomotives have a serious effect on the
overall economics of the line.

The fourth and last alternative, again well-known overseas, is to gain extra height by a spiral or helicoidal location. This is the most elaborate of the possibilities, consisting of laying out a circle or circuit on a rising grade, which finally crosses over itself, at a height which represents the gain of altitude won.

As has already been mentioned, before Gerald Fox took charge (he graduated at Cambridge in 1960), two alignments had already been designed and estimates made in connection with the claim against the CEGB for complete restitution. The earlier one, dating from January, 1958, was by Charles Goode (running round the west side of the lake) and the other was the ultimate in acceptability, by consulting engineers (and railway specialists) Livesay & Henderson in September 1958. This went round the east side of the proposed lake and crossed the new dam. Both schemes involved quite long tunnels and steepening the ruling grade of the line from 1 in 75 to 1 in 60. The second scheme took into account the Electricity people's rather surprising refusal to allow a railway to cross the hillside behind the new power station. On the other hand, on the face of it equally surprisingly, there was no objection on their part to a railway crossing the proposed dam. This was in fact due to the forethought of Joseph Ballantyne-Dykes, a partner of the Livesay & Henderson firm. He made the designers of the dam make provision for a narrow-gauge railway running across its crest, underlining his request by reminding them of the notorious Crichell Down case, in which a minister had to resign and no doubt several other public servants were sent to the Civil Service equivalent of Siberia.

This Gerald Fox, then, managed to persuade the Festiniog Board to invite him to investigate the terrain with the idea of finding a route appropriate to a crazy notion which he and a few other engineering graduates had, of employing a volunteer force to construct the new line. In Jugoslavia major railway construction had been undertaken by an international force of volunteers, but Gerald was not aware of this; the idea was original thinking on his part.

Early in 1962, Gerald Fox first began doodling on an Ordinance Survey 2½in to the mile (1 : 25,000 scale) contoured map, in order to establish possible routes. Tunnel construction (as needed for the 'Goode' and 'Livesay & Henderson' routes) was considered to be outside the scope of volunteers, so his intentions were to find a route which did not need one, or at worst, only a short one.

The first route considered on the map looped round Rhoslyn Lake at Dduallt, doubled back above the existing line as far as Campbell's Siding, then turned north through a pass to the west of Moel Dduallt. The pass would have needed deepening quite considerably, but once through, easy construction down the Ystradau Valley would have followed, with the possibility of going either side of the new lake. The idea was rejected on the grounds that the amount of new construction was far more than on the other routes considered.

Another solution was to veer slightly right (instead of sharp left) beyond Dduallt and build a shelf on the dubious scree-covered slopes of the mountain (Moel Ystradau) to the east of the lake. It could then cross the valley over the new dam. However, a low saddle by Brooke's Quarry was discovered – it was not clearly shown on the 2½in map – and this seemed to offer the possibility of a less hazardous alternative.

To reach this saddle from Dduallt, all the four alternatives mentioned (looping, switch-backing, steepening and spiralling) were considered and finally, after all, it was decided that on all practical and economic grounds a spiral location around Dduallt and Rhoslyn Lake had advantages. For some reason and for a long time it had been assumed that a precipice continued into the woods here, which would have precluded such a solution. The first spiral tried encircled the old tunnel mouth, but had rather excessive earth-works.

Any doodles that looked promising had of course to be confirmed on the ground. A major survey is not a thing to be undertaken lightly, but Gerald and his friends put their time and skill liberally at the Company's disposal, coming up week-end after week-end with a Land-Rover, instruments and equipment. Accommodation was usually available at the Cae'r Blaidd Youth Hostel in Llan Festiniog. In all, 10 week-ends early in 1963 were spent in Wales, with between 8 and 12 people on site taking measurements and readings. For each sortie many hours would be spent plotting the survey. The result of over a year's work was a series of contoured survey sheets to a scale of 50 inches to the mile.

A Land-Rover was used to get on to the ground, while theodolites and levels were hired. Incidentally, these two types of survey appliance are often confused; the theodolite is the king of instruments and, if set up at one point, can be used to measure angles, both horizontally and vertically, between that point and two other points. It can also be used to measure distances. A level (which looks rather similar to a theodolite and is often referred to as such by laymen) is much simpler and can do one thing only – that is to set up a precisely level line of sight. A surveyor normally peers through it and takes the reading of the horizontal hair-line against a 'staff', which is held vertically with its foot on the ground at some distant point whose level is needed to be known. The staff could be described as a big ruler, with provision for extension to 15ft or so. The use of these instruments is tediously slow but strangely satisfying, especially amongst beautiful scenery and in a good cause.

The new route then, turned sharp right at Dduallt station and continued doing so until it had crossed back on itself. Finally, after over 360 degrees of curvature, it was running more or less parallel with the original course, but some 30ft higher up. Further on, the new route curved right again, crossed above the southern portal of the old tunnel and then swung left through a new but vestigial tunnel near Brooke's Quarry, to reach the top of the new dam. This new route became known as the East Shore Route and was the one adopted at the beginning of design and construction.

Finally (as Fox says in a 'discussion' published in the

Festiniog Railway Magazine for Winter 1973/4), much excited, 'I wrote (Festiniog Director) Leslie Smith a letter saying that there was a route graded at 1 in 80 possible, with a spiral at Dduallt and a 1 in 60 route based on steepening the old line back to Campbell's and what did the Company think? The directors said they thought the spiral sounded excellent and we worked on that ever after'.

In the proper manner, the ruling gradient of 1 in 80 was compensated for curvature, that is the grade was reduced in severity to compensate for the extra friction on the curves:

Curve radius	Maximum gradient
400ft	1 in 85
300ft	1 in 90
200ft	1 in 110

Incidentally, on the old line, which was designed for gravity trains, compensation tended to be the other way; grades were made *steeper* on the curves to *allow* for the extra friction. All curves were entered gently by transition curves and a formation width of 8ft was allowed for throughout. Later this had to be increased to 10ft.

By another happy chance it turned out that the early stages of construction would also suit something akin to the original 'Goode' route running round the west shore of the new lake. Long after construction had begun, in fact in 1969, the CEGB finally relented and allowed the West Shore Route, thought to be less expensive, but including a 284m tunnel and to which the Dduallt spiral location could be married. One must confess to a tinge of regret here that they did so, for the location on the dam and the viaducts over the spillways would have been very fine, while tunnels by their very nature, hide all the work, effort and money that goes into making them. The bridge-works also being more predictable than tunnelling might not in the end have proved so much more expensive.

The author, who had too many turgid experiences inside railway tunnels during British Rail's steamy and smoky days, admits to a prejudice against them. This feeling was certainly

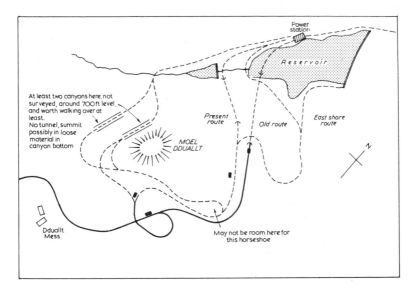

Fig. 3. ... almost instantly from Ffriskers (San Francisco) came a Ffox doodle suggesting an alternative Grand Canyon route ... *FR Civil Engineering Group*

shared by Gerald Fox (and now possibly by other FR people), because when in 1968 news reached him of the West Shore Route with its long tunnel, almost instantly from what he called 'Ffriskers' (San Francisco) came a Ffox doodle – reproduced herewith – suggesting either an alternative Grand Canyon route round the back of Moel Dduallt, or a further wobble to the east before going round the west side of the lake. Either would have been very fine scenically and almost totally volunteerable (if that is a word), although in the case of the former, a small amount of work already done at Barn, Midge and Rosary would have been lost. Of course, both the routes would have been rather longer than the one finally adopted.

Gerald said to Mike Schumann, 'I do not think volunteers would be any good at mucking out a long tunnel . . . the fumes, lack of fresh air and scenery and the extreme dullness of digging out 7,000 cu yd would scare off all but you and I – and if you look after the messes, it will take me just over 100 years, plus time spent out of the country or on round the world trips'.

Incidentally, talking of communications between Gerald Fox and Mike Schumann, his eventual successor, the letter recruiting Mike, then a student at Cambridge, has survived. It appears to have been written in the Spring of 1963 . . .

31A Upper Park Road
London N.W. 3

Dear Mike,

Thank you for your letter. We could indeed do with your help as we are now engaged in full-scale design of the new line. There is indeed a spiral, at Rhoslyn, and the ruling gradient of the new line is 1 in 80. We have to get an estimate out by June 18th and are pretty pushed. You cannot, of course, work in the office during the day, but Peter Jamieson's flat, where I am now living, is fully equipped, and we can get anything you need in the way of drawing gear. Suggest you come to my office on Tuesday evening at 6.30 and I can put you in the picture. Then you can either stay in London for the night with us or at home (I can take you home) or take a drawing or two to Cambridge, and work on it there. If you stay in London you can work in the flat during the day. Is there anyone else among the railway and engineers in Cambridge who can show up on occasions for the next fortnight? Suggest you ring me up either at the flat around or after midnight on Monday or at MAY 8636 during Tuesday. Expenses of this sort are recoverable. Many thanks for your offer – look forward to seeing you.

Yours
(signed) Gerald

One point about these Fox versions of the West Side Route as well as the East Side ones is that the longer distances and running times compared with the one finally adopted would have meant more costly operation. More fuel, drivers' time and, in the limit, rolling stock would be needed. Mike Schumann took this into account when plumping for the tunnel; perhaps a little unfairly (in the writer's view) no corresponding account was taken of the additional drawing power of more scenic routes as well as (which is another way of

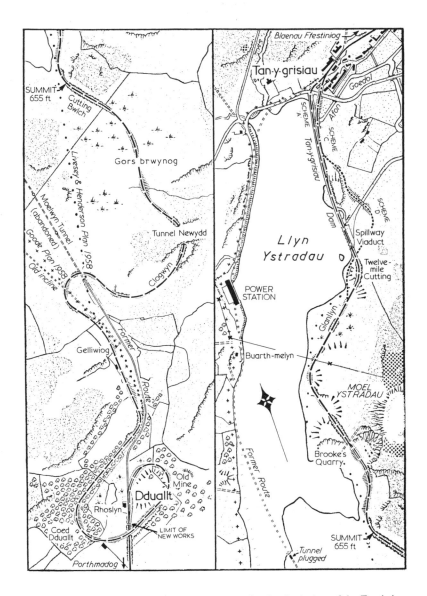

Fig 4 The originally agreed east shore route for the deviation of the Festiniog Railway. It was never finally resolved whether the line was to run actually on the dam or (as shown dotted) whether a separate viaduct was to have been provided. *Festiniog Railway*

saying the same thing) increased fares for the longer distance.

Returning to the East Shore Route, however, various schemes were prepared by Gerald Fox and his collaborators to cross the valley on or near the dam, as shown by the artist's impressions herewith. Scheme A was the route across the dam but there were problems with access ducts – needing removable sections of track – and possible difficulties with the Ministry of Transport (as it then was) over the level crossing. Scheme B involved a bridge over the road, while schemes C and D involved alignments partly off and wholly off the dam crest respectively. The landscaping experts then said that a dam and a railway viaduct running separately across the valley would spoil their aesthetics, so it sounded as though Scheme A might be the one after all. Automatic road barriers would have solved the level crossing problem and no doubt the ducts problem could have been overcome. Or, since the world-famous (and local) architect Sir Clough Williams-Ellis had interested himself in the project on the Festiniog's behalf – no one could possibly take him on when it came to aesthetics – the viaduct might have been agreed to anyway. What a monument it would have been to the Deviation project as well, of course, as being a superb advertisement for the Railway.

Another reason for some to regret the abandonment of the East Shore Route lies in the enormous amount of work that went into preparing some 50 large and complex drawings to full professional standards. At modest consultancy rates and in present day money, Gerald Fox and his associates put into the project a sum well into five figures. Their names (Mike Elvy, A. F. Farthing, R. A. B. Hall, Peter Jamieson, G. J. Keleher, G. A. Pinfold, D. A. H. Richmond, Mike Schumann and A. B. Stanier) should be remembered with gratitude. Several will recur during this narrative. In all, some 50 people gave their time to the survey and design work.

The new 'Schumann' route which was finally adopted was also the result of a certain amount of horse-trading with the CEGB. The first suggestion put to them involved a 1600ft

Above: The cause of it all – the CEGB's lower storage reservoir at Tan-y-Grisiau seen here in June 1965. The power station is on the far shore of the lake and the originally planned deviation route lay parallel to or across the top of the dam. In the foreground is the surviving line on to Blaenau Ffestiniog. *M. Luck*

Below: Surveyors at work: a level is set up by the old footbridge at Gelliwiog. *Dan Wilson*

Above: Cutting the first sod of the Deviation near Dduallt on 2 January 1965.
Mike Schumann
Below: The first sod site after three months' work. The material dug from the
cutting on the left has been used to form the embankment on the right, transport
being provided by the hopper wagon and track shown. *Dan Wilson*

tunnel inclined at 1 in 130, and passed close behind the power station. It was then decided to steepen and shorten the tunnel to 1000ft and run the railway across the hillside some 30ft above the power station. There were to be hidden bridges across the penstock pipes. A cutting was then followed by level crossings over the penstock and Stwlan dam roads respectively. The route ran behind the CEGB reception centre, crossed the Afon Cwmorthin by a concrete bridge and finally joined the old route at Tan-y-Grisiau. There was room there for a fine S-shaped station, complete with island platform loop to handle 12-coach trains. Mike Schumann and the Junta had only five weeks in which to prepare an outline scheme for this final alignment.

Having mentioned the starting-point of the Deviation several times already, a problem which will here affect most readers – at least the non-Welsh – is the question of how to begin from a place you cannot even begin to pronounce. Now Dduallt means Black-Hill . . . for 'Dd' substitute 'Th', and for 'u' substitute a short English 'e'. Then all you have to do is to roll the double 'l' with a kind of 'h'l', so phonetically, 'Ddu-allt' equals 'The-ah'lt'. Irreverent people say you should pronounce as if bringing up phlegm . . . More fun than just saying Blackhill!

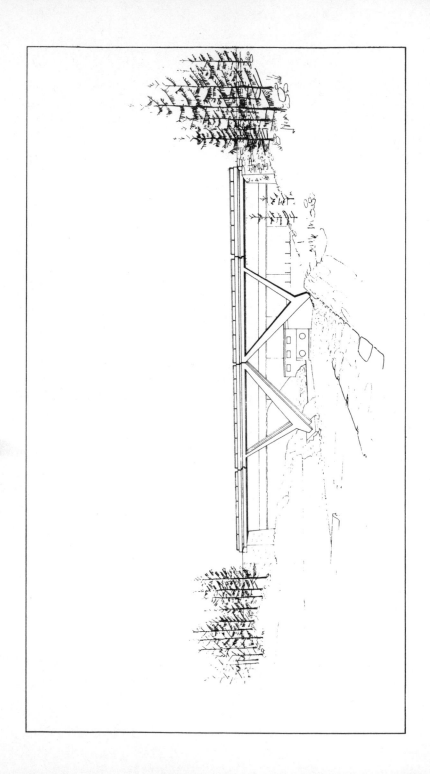

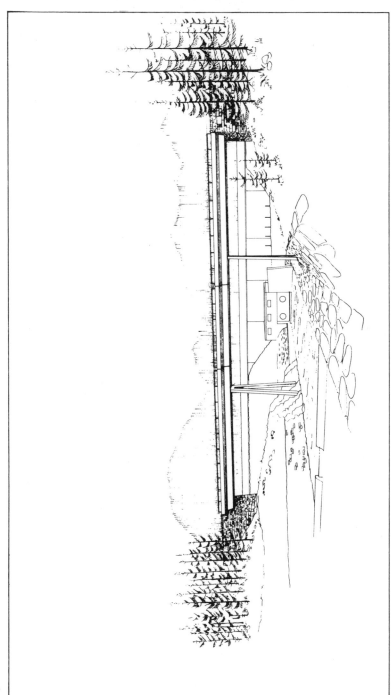

Fig 5 Perspective views of two designs for Llyn Ystradau viaduct on the proposed east shore route. *Peter Jamieson*

4
Light railway orders

'If he were
To be made honest by an act of Parliament,
I should not alter in my faith of him'
Ben Johnson   The Devil is an Ass

Once a route of a railway has been decided, it is usually (but not always) necessary to obtain parliamentary powers to build it. Before the Light Railways Act of 1896 it was necessary to have a private Act of Parliament – the Festiniog originally had to have its own, as has been mentioned – but since then a statutory instrument of parliamentary authority called a Light Railway Order (LRO) has been available. The procedure for this is much less fraught and cumbersome than any private Act of Parliament could be, although it is still fairly lengthy.

The reason for all this palaver is that railway builders usually need compulsory powers to buy (or have rights over) at least some of the land needed for the line. One also needs statutory powers, for example, where the line is to cross the Queen's Highway, whether above, below or on the level. There have been many cases of 'non-statutory' railways in Britain, in which it has been possible to build the line just by agreement with whoever owns the land, but except for the first 400yd of the new line round the spiral, this was not one of them. In fact, before the FR reaches the grand new station in the centre of Blaenau Ffestiniog, it will have had to have gone through the Light Railway mill three or four times.

Every conceivable detail of the line has to be included in the application to the Department of Transport – plans and sections, of course, but also things like the cost of fencing and telegraph poles. The people to whom details are to be sent include all local authorities in the area, together with a long list of such diverse bodies as the Post Office, Ministry of Defence and Ministry of Agriculture. Notices in prescribed form must be served on all the owners and occupiers of lands affected by the new line and a book of reference made available for public inspection. Newspaper advertisements etc must appear.

The story of the Festiniog Railway (Light Railway) (Amendment) orders 1968 and 1975 was told by Leslie Smith (typically playing down his own part in what was a most tiresome, long drawn-out and difficult affair), in the *Festiniog Railway Magazine* for Spring, 1976:

'Bloody Mary', Queen of England (it is said) maintained that when she died the word Calais would be found engraved on her heart, and I have no doubt that so far as I am concerned there will be two names on mine, one a Welsh farmer and the other one of our nationalized industries. I have known them both for so many years that it is unthinkable and unlikely that contact will ever be lost. I first met the aforementioned farmer when Alan Pegler, Trevor Bailey and I first visited the line and at Tan y Grisiau hired a FR wagon (for 2/6) which careered, with the three of us aboard, out of control, into the inky and damp depths of Moelwyn tunnel. The nationalized industry came a little later but the various skirmishes ranging from the House of Lords, Court of Appeal, Lands Tribunal, Public Inquiries, etc, have left their marks.

The two Light Railway Orders made in 1968 and 1975 are amendments to the principal Order of 1923. Light Railway Orders are Statutory Instruments, that is, they are made under provisions of Acts of Parliament which authorise them and in respect of which Regulations are made which govern their manner and content. The 1923 Order, apart from, as it were, downgrading the railway, authorised the construction of a connection with the Welsh Highland Railway and a new station. The railway, as authorised by its 1832 Act, is known as Railway No 1, the connecting line with the Welsh Highland was Railway No 2. The

deviation line from Dduallt to Brookes' Quarry, authorised by the
1968 Light Railway Order, is known as Railway No 3, whilst the
later Light Railway Order authorises the construction of Railway
No 4.

Looking back, the 1968 Order was the most difficult. We had
instructed Parliamentary Agents, Messrs. Sharpe, Pritchard & Co,
and Mr Hardinge Pritchard of that firm, a most able and
exceedingly patient friend, has guided us through the mass of
regulations, negotiations and requirements that go to make the
Orders.

Work on the 1968 Light Railway Order commenced in 1964.
Gerald Fox had produced his scheme for a route around the east
side of the reservoir via Brookes' Quarry and the CEGB dam. The
great snag was that by using the dam the railway would be within
the operational limits of the Power Station and also the dam was at
that time open to the public. It is said the Queen herself dedicated
the top of the dam as a public footpath at the opening. It is not
difficult to envisage the disruption to train services which could
have resulted if the CEGB had wanted occupation of the dam or if
crowds of visitors were wandering about. The CEGB obviously
had some idea that the trains only ran when required and it was
difficult to convince their legal officers that regular services were
already in operation and would need to be maintained when
through running between Portmadoc and Blaenau Ffestiniog
commenced. One could also imagine the reaction of the Railway
Inspectorate if trains were to mingle with pedestrians on such
limited width as the dam provided. The more one thought about
it the greater the difficulties became from the operating point of
view, so we prepared various schemes, taking the railway along
the down stream side of the dam. These met with objections from
the CEGB landscape consultant which, in fact, were never resolved.
So, although planning approval had been obtained for the whole
east side route it was decided that it would be prudent to limit the
Light Railway Order authorisation to a point short of the dam and
Brookes' Quarry was chosen. I was hopeful that eventually the
CEGB would relent and agree to the west side route for the dispute
over the dam crossing had highlighted the absolute necessity for
the railway to be completely separated from any operational
feature of the Power Station.

Our Parliamentary Agents prepared the draft order, plans were
submitted, amended and re-submitted, re-amended and re-
submitted, and negotiations were attempted with the landowners

concerned. There were three in number and they all objected to the draft order. Efforts were made to satisfy the objections, but a public inquiry was held at which agreement was reached on the safeguards for each owner which are carefully set out in articles 8 and 9 of the Order.

The 1968 Order as made gave the Festiniog Railway Company powers to acquire the land required compulsorily but efforts were made to purchase by agreement. One of the private landowners agreed to sell his land by agreement, a price was agreed and the deviationists got to work. The other landowner referred the matter to the Lands Tribunal who determined the compensation payable. No land owned by the CEGB was affected at this stage.

The safeguards for the landowners' protection include cattle and sheep creeps, a level crossing at Gelliwiog, and prohibition of facilities for passengers to board or alight from trains on land they (the landowners) formerly owned. Another requirement was that the Company had to notify the owners at the commencement of each year of the programme of works to be followed during that year. The protection clause for the CEGB which had taken such a long time to prepare and agree was never, in the event, necessary. Efforts to persuade the CEGB that the railway could operate along the west side of the reservoir and around the back of the Power Station were eventually successful. Mike Schumann prepared the necessary drawings, unconditional planning permission was, after much legal argument, obtained and the draft Order prepared. After an initial objection, agreement was reached with the private landowners affected who withdrew their objection and this only left the CEGB. Many hours were spent in preparing and agreeing their protective clause, and when this was at last achieved there was a further delay because certain re-drafting of the Order was necessary owing to the change of heart over a station being sited on CEGB land. There was argument too about the number of trains passing over the level crossings and also the limits of the new line which could be built by the Deviationists. The change of heart over the station necessitated a further planning application with all the delays associated with such matters and which, in this case, were exacerbated by local government reorganisation. The clause providing protection for the CEGB is extremely long; it has 19 sub-sections, many of which are sub-divided. No deviation from the route shown on the detailed drawings is allowed (normally limits of deviation are permitted so as to allow slight route amendments to be made if necessary). There are restrictions on use of

CEGB roads and many other matters to which careful attention has to be given at all times.

Eventually the CEGB withdrew its objection to the draft order. As there were only two landowners concerned, both of whom had withdrawn their objections, it was not necessary to have a public inquiry and after clearing a few matters with the Department of the Environment the 1975 order was laid before Parliament and approved.

A lot of the hassle was excessively tedious and extended, but there were moments. For example, at the public enquiry into the 1968 order (held on 26 and 27 January, 1967), Joseph Ballantyne-Dykes relates how, during the earlier enquiry, he was cross-examined by the nephew of David Lloyd George (no less), a partner in the Porthmadog firm of solicitors then known as Lloyd George and George. After a refusal to give an instant opinion on the engineering feasibility of some alternative, George said 'and you call yourself an expert'. The answer, 'Yes, it is just because I am an expert that I do refuse'.

The actual text of the significant clauses making up the two Light Railway Orders, as finally issued, are given in Appendix B. The material omitted deals entirely with legal technicalities.

Once a Light Railway Order is granted it is still not the end of government involvement. As things stand now, any railway of gauge 15in or more, whether 'statutory' (ie with parliamentary powers) or not, before it can be used for the carriage of farepaying passengers, must be passed as safe on completion by HM Chief Inspecting Officer of Railways. Attempts have been made in the past to avoid this by such dodges as carrying passengers free, but charging for their shopping baskets. Recently there have been cases of preserved steam concerns who allow only members to ride, but offer instant day membership at a small fee.

Of course, such practices are not the way of the (picking one's words very carefully) world's oldest independent public railway company still operating trains. Indeed, whatever may be the case elsewhere in Government, the present railway inspectorate takes endless pains to be regarded by the smaller railways as a friend and counsellor rather than an aloof schoolmaster complete with mortar-board and cane.

Planning permission is a pre-requisite of any Light Railway Order but in the Festiniog Railway's case the fact that the proposal was limited to the involuntary relocation of a long-existing railway made the outcome less in doubt. However, one notes an attempt by a certain County official to have planning permission refused simply in order to save a little embarrassment to his fellow officials who, never imagining that the railway would re-open, had taken away a bridge further up the line and raised the road level there.

So, with 'bogey' for the course of obtaining a Light Railway Order being three years, a great debt of gratitude is due to Mr Evershed, a Festiniog Railway Society member, who was able to arrange for a concern known as the Economic Forestry Group to present the company with the piece of land needed for the first 400yd of the Deviation. Work could therefore begin and experience could be gained several years before possession could be taken of the main corridor of land needed.

5

First sod and afterwards

' "Law, Brer Tarrypin!" sez Brer Fox, sezee, "you
ain't seen no trouble yit, ef you wanter see sho' nuff
trouble, you des oughter go 'longer me; I'm de man
w'at kin show you trouble," sezee.'
Joel Chandler Harris   Uncle Remus

So the stage was set, the route chosen, enough land acquired to
make a start, an engineer was in the saddle, a little money was
in the till and a faithful few were eager to begin. Accordingly,
in a field close to Dduallt Station, on Saturday, 2 January, 1965
at 3 pm, lots were drawn for the honour of cutting the first sod.
It fell to Doctor Michael Lewis of Cambridge University to
set the great project in motion, using a specially provided (and
nearly left behind) gold-painted spade. By the end of Sunday,
12yd of formation were complete and a side-tipping wagon was
being used. The following members of what was now being
called the Civil Engineering Group were present; Fox himself,
of course, and Peter Jamieson (who made so many of the
Deviation drawings), John Collier, John Carter, Paul
Bradshaw and Moragh Walker (later Moragh Bradshaw and
the first lady of the Deviation in more ways than one); Mike
Schumann, another Cambridge engineer, who later on was to
master-mind the tunnel and other major works was there; also
Dan Wilson, whose brilliant wit still delights (and occasionally
confounds) readers of his editorials in the *Festiniog Railway
Magazine*. Jonathan Tyler (at present chairman of the Ecology
party) and Jim Foster made up the ten-strong group.

Those who were *not* there (often more significant than those
who were) included local dignitaries and the top brass of the

railway. While this was to the taste of the Deviationists – mainly because all those present would at once set to with picks and shovels – this isolationism was to cause difficulties, as we shall see.

A word on the basic principles of railway construction is perhaps now in order. Except that constructors nowadays have bigger buckets and spades these principles have remained unchanged since George Stephenson's time and before. In order to make a grade suitable for a railway, the natural lie of the land has to be modified either by digging down to lower it or by tipping material to raise it. These two operations are usually complimentary so one goes, as the Deviationists did on that day, to a point where a 'cutting' changes into an 'embankment'. Then one starts digging the cutting, and tipping what has been dug to form the embankment. A vehicle is required which has a tipping body; ideally it should be possible to tip both to the side and to the front. This is done best by having both a side-tipper and an end-tipper.

At first there is only a short distance to go from cutting to embankment and a wheelbarrow, say, can be used, but soon enough the distance becomes greater and something better is needed. Before modern rubber-tyred earth-moving equipment was available this would mean (and in the Festiniog case, did mean) a tramway on which tipping wagons or skips could easily be moved. While the works are shallow, progress is rapid; indeed, that little group in that first week-end had no difficulty in completing 12yd of formation. As cutting and embankment deepen, not only does the amount of material increase disproportionately, but also it has to be carried much further. Similar working groups later on would find that each skip load was only advancing the grade half an inch or so!

This nice simple process is complicated by two things. First, in mountain country rock is seldom far below the surface of the ground and this rock needs shattering into small pieces before it can be moved. The normal process used is to drill quite deep holes, using an air-driven percussion drill powered by an air

45

compressor; cylindrical sticks of explosive are placed in the holes. Modern explosives are quite safe to handle; in fact they are only likely to be set off by another explosion. To set a charge off then, one fixes a detonator in contact with the explosive. This is a small tube containing a tiny amount of a really sensitive explosive, which (according to type) can be fired either electrically or by a fuse. On the Deviation the charges forming each blast were connected by an instantaneous fuse known as Cordtex. The Cordtex was itself set off by detonator in which was inserted a short length of slow-burning fuse; this enabled the firer to get clear.

To ensure that the end result is a neat pile of small rocks rather than a few widely scattered large ones, a number of charges arranged in a particular pattern have to be fired simultaneously. It is important to be certain that all the charges forming a blast have in fact gone off before digging begins.

The second complication arises from the fact that the material one digs out at the beginning, ie the top soil, is the one that is really best to be tipped last, to clad the otherwise rather bald slopes of new embankments and cuttings. It is often necessary to put the top soil aside for use later.

The week-end following 'first sod' was less euphoric. Those recorded as being present were 'G.D.F.', Mike Schumann and Jim Foster again, plus someone called Adrian. Moragh brought her sister Joan and there were three other girls (Liz Williams, Gill Hopkins and Sue). 'It rained as it can only rain in North Wales and never stopped'. Work proceeded in laying the concrete floor of the new mess and 'it was discovered that English women do not make such good coolies'. A 'well-wisher' had systematically moved all the survey pegs and markers as well as pushing the skip over the end of the line and down a steep place. The police had to be informed. The party returned with relief to their youth hostel in Llan Ffestiniog on Saturday night although 'the mud slide down the hill in the pitch dark was not enjoyed by all'.

There are all sorts of things to explain about this; first, we see

Gerald Fox's position as leader nicely acknowledged through reference to him in the log by initials and not by name, and second, the equal participation of women, a thing very rare in the railway restoration world. The sabotage was again just typical of things that do happen on civil engineering projects; the gentleman concerned no doubt thought the group were just grown-up children rather than dedicated adults led by experienced professional surveyors. The visible pegs were just put back beside the secret ones (pipes driven into the ground) which were the master marks. Lastly, of course, the new mess must be mentioned.

Colonel Andrew Campbell, late of the Black Watch, since 1963 had lived in the ancient eleventh century Dduallt Manor House, just below the Festiniog Railway's line and about half a mile from the site of the 'first sod' location. So far from protesting or hindering the Deviationists, he welcomed them even to the extent of providing a barn to convert to a mess. He also possessed a 'licence to store explosives' and had had experience in their use. In this area also he was prepared to offer assistance. 'Cast your bread upon the waters' says the Good Book and in this case and in due course the railway returned it with interest by providing a siding at the Manor and allowing the Colonel running powers to Tan-y-Bwlch station for his private train. The Manor house had then no proper road access. Also, of course, in due time he got back a barn converted into habitable living quarters. Even so, Andrew Campbell's name comes high up when the Deviationists count their benefactors. The conversion of the barn began in October following a series of week-ends spent rebuilding the parapet walls of the Cei Mawr embankment below Tan-y-Bwlch.

On some occasions during these early days just before the barn was ready, Mrs Campbell even had small parties to stay in her house. Moragh Bradshaw relates how just before Easter she achieved two life-long ambitions – to sleep in a four-poster bed and work a pneumatic drill. Over that Easter the Dduallt Mess was first occupied with (as the account in the Dduallt Site

Record Book reads) 'the fantastic sight of bodies carrying mattresses, pots, beds, etc across the mountain from an eleven-truck train hauled by *Moelwyn* (*Moelwyn* is an ex-War Department rail tractor). A party of 15 (all except 4 male) was present; the first mess account reveals receipts of £39 10s 0d (£39.50) at 10s (50p) per head per night) and expenditure of £37 7s 2½d (£37.36).

The first compressor (borrowed from Col Campbell) also arrived in time for Easter; so, for the first time, it was possible to bore holes into Wales, fill them with explosives and so rive her apart. Until then, when rock was encountered, it had been a question of fighting a losing battle by chipping away with picks and hammers. Alas, when the first company compressor came the Deviationists were to learn that (in those days anyway), old plant was usually only disposed of when it was beyond being made to work properly.

The first blast was fired on that Friday afternoon, 16 April under Colonel Campbell's direction, but was not too successful. Someone has actually over-written the entry in the log with the words 'no marks for tact', unnecessarily so because rock, being natural material, needs some trial and error before successful blasting can be achieved. A second blast on Saturday was fine. It is also noted that 'spectators were persuaded to leave us by some suggestion of their wielding a shovel'.

The Colonel did all the Deviation blasting at this period and he always took his collie dog Flash with him. Flash always realised that shot firing was dangerous and had to be forcibly restrained when the Colonel went to light the fuse.

One evening he had fired a round of holes on Barn Site; it had achieved just what we wanted, ie cracking the rock and loosening it as opposed to spreading it all over Merioneth. The Colonel decided to dismantle the rock face with a crowbar for a minute or two. He was still at it over an hour later and his wife Mary on seeing the colour of his face caused by his exertions became very concerned.

In fact, crow-barring a rock face is one of the most satisfying

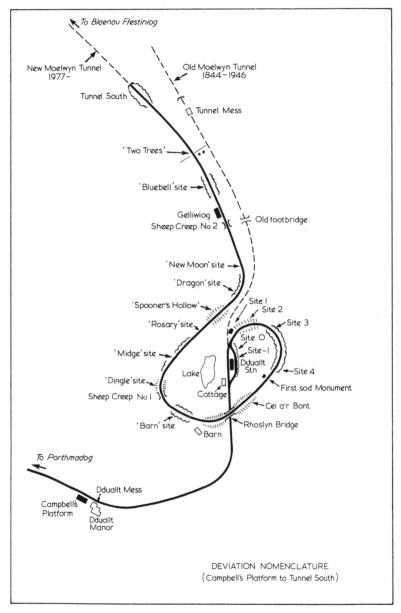

Fig 6 Deviation nomenclature from Campbell's platform to Tunnel South.

experiences known on the 'Dev'; given a bit of promotion it would make a good Olympics event, being very rewarding for the participant and an excellent spectator sport.

Around this time Gerald Fox had co-opted four others to assist him in the direction of the project. In due time this group became known as 'The Junta'. They were to meet regularly in London; Jimmy's Restaurant in Frith Street and The Grapes in Carnaby Street (both, alas, now no more) were the scenes of great decision-taking. Strangely enough it appears that the formal Junta meetings tended to turn out to be rather lesser occasions. The first Junta consisted of Paul Bradshaw, solicitor (Cambridge), Peter Jamieson, civil engineer (Cambridge), Roger Simons, civil engineer, and Mike Schumann, civil engineer (Cambridge).

After Easter a group of students from King's College, London, wrote that their study of 'social science and theology brought new light to bear upon living conditions and work situations in this particular mess – religious services had of necessity to be temporarily suspended in favour of the more irksome necessities of life in this unusual situation'. But 'shopping expeditions, *contrary to Foxy's instructions*, were daily and lengthy'. Author's italics. They finished up a page of philosophising with two pertinent comments – (a) 'a flushing wc in a mess is an absolute essential' and (b) 'for the mountains and terrific scenery Deo Gratias'.

Often (with a few honourable exceptions) the verbosity of entries in the log was in inverse ratio to the work done on site. The following party just wrote: 'Slept, dug, ate, slept, dug and went home.' No latin tags for them! The next big event was in fact the opening of that wc on Whit Sunday. It was not recorded who was the first customer.

One of the many Fox doctrines was to be unenthusiastic about having railway enthusiasts on the deviation. Small wonder when the temptation of one of the world's premier narrow-gauge railway spectacles was only a few miles away. He was not, however, above indulging his own railway fancies. . . .

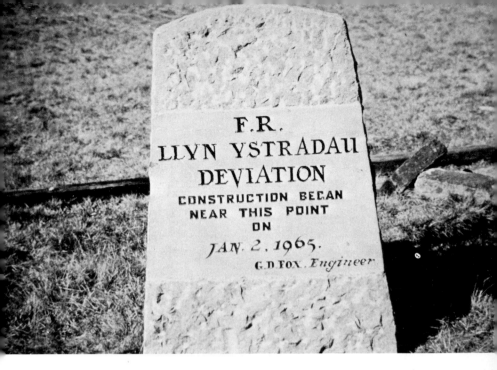

Above: The stone which today marks the historic spot where construction of the deviation began. *FR Civil Engineering Group*

Below: The interior of Dduallt or Bottom mess; the kitchen is in the corner. Of the sign on the wall little more need be said other than that Gerald Fox worked on the reconstruction of Oxford Circus station. On one occasion the sign was set up at the FR halt nearby and a suitably bowler-hatted and umbrella'd group of deviationists joined the train to the astonishment of the tourists. *Norman Gurley*

Above: Dduallt station in June 1967 with the original line from Porthmadog to Blaenau Ffestiniog, through the old Moelwyn tunnel, on the right. *M. Luck*
Below: The lowest section of the spiral at Dduallt begins to take shape. The view is of site 1 from site 2 before the two met. The photograph was taken on 6 June 1967. The original FR line can be seen passing through the trees on the left-hand side of the picture just behind the new embankment. *M. Luck*

Not having rolled down the Vale of Ffestiniog since 1939 (at least), and certainly no part of the restoration scheme were the legendary gravity slate trains – the ones for which the railway was originally constructed. A no-show digging party from the Wylfa nuclear power station site in Anglesey (Gerald Fox had recently taken up an appointment there) gave two or three of the faithful the opportunity to send a skip down for modification that way. The ten miles took $1\frac{3}{4}$ hours – with some pushing on the sharp curves below Tan-y-Bwlch. The usual single-line tablet system was dispensed with and safety taken care of by an American style train order. . . .

SATURDAY 19*th* *JUNE*, 1965
FROM 6 p.m. to 12 MIDNIGHT ALL SECTIONS NORTH OF PEN COB JUNCTION ARE IN POSSESSION OF G. FOX TO WORK TROLLEY SOUTH TO BOSTON LODGE FROM T-y-B.

P. A. Dukes

(Paul Dukes was then and is still in charge of the Company's Boston Lodge Works near Porthmadog.)

Although he had the right piece of paper on this occasion, Gerald Fox had a slight tendency to be casual over the running of trolleys. It was back in 1957, before the line was opened to Tan-y-Bwlch, that a Fox trolley run nearly collided with a works train and convinced Manager Allan Garraway that Volunteer Fox, who had only recently left school, still needed a school-master. Fortunately there was one to hand in the person of Keith Catchpole, whose famous troupe of boys (the 'Tadpoles' – fifty strong that year) from The Chase School, Enfield, were then engaged in clearing a train-sized hole through the rhododendron woods. The cockney boys thought that public-school Gerald (in pork-pie hat complete with feather) was a great figure of fun – vice versa, too, of course – and they enjoyed each other's company for a hilarious fortnight. Another (and potentially more serious) trolley incident involving GDF is remembered in song – see Appendix D, *No Brake On My Trolley*.

Another facet of the Fox character was quick repartee. A local farmer appeared one day and stated that the line would only be completed 'over his dead body'. Says Fox, 'Mr Bradshaw here is a solicitor, he could help you with your will'. On the other hand, more than some of the others, Gerald had great patience with local people. The traditional approach to serious business hereabouts is via a long conversation on all manner of other things. Richard Burton, the actor, once said that in Wales only second rate entertainers go professional – so such conversations are likely to be fun. But they are also liable to be time-consuming and thus exasperating to Anglo-Saxons late on a Sunday evening, watching their estimated time of arrival in London receding into the small hours. Like the others, Gerald also had to be at work by 9 am, but he never begrudged these valuable hours spent with the railway's neighbours to be. Incidentally, dislike for the re-opening of the railway never got in the way of a hospitable welcome on their part.

Gerald Fox did not base his system of leadership on that of the noble Duke of Plaza Toro; he led from the front and worked just that little bit harder and more tirelessly than anyone else. His enthusiasms led the Deviationists a bit astray sometimes, but they followed him through thick and thin. For example, the use of canopies to keep rain (and occasionally sun) off the diggers was not really found practical, nor did the use of 'small smoky fires' to discourage the midges get tried very often.

In principle, however, his methods have stood the test of time and been fully vindicated, but not everyone agreed with his use of early Victorian railway building methods. Consultants Livesay & Henderson condemned them in scathing terms; for example, embankments, they said, should be built up in layers, each one consolidated as it was laid, using modern plant. Tipping the banks straight away to full height (as is implicit in the Victorian method) was all wrong. Whatever may be the rights and wrongs of this as a general theory, in this particular case, where rocky fill rather than peat was used, the embankments have in fact proved reasonably stable; now the 'alternative technology' methods used to make them are thought to be the 'in' thing for roads and railways built in third-world countries, just as they used to be in the days of the British Empire.

One simple Victorian device was the shovelling board. Anyone knows how much easier it is to shovel off a floor rather than directly from a heap of, say, coal. Well, a shovelling board is simply a portable piece of floor made of timber or sheet steel. For details of Victorian excavation techniques, see page 182.

Talking of technology, a step away from the early days of railway construction was taken during the first week of August when a Schmeidag light bulldozer was briefly borrowed from the Wylfa site. It was small enough to reach the site by narrow-gauge train but, alas, this smallness meant insufficient power to deal with other than top-soil or similar soft material. So the 13-strong group of human diggers (who included a hi-jacked hitch-hiker who had injudiciously thumbed a lift on the A5 road on the Friday night) had no reason to fear idleness. Hot water reached the taps in the mess that week and a shower was commissioned. The 'mileage' of new grade now exceeded 100yd.

Bank Holiday-Weekend in August was 'energetic and successful'. End tippers were introduced for the first time and this greatly eased the extension of embankments. A 'borrowed' air-driven pump was available to pump out the upper end of the partly completed cutting. Gas cooking replaced paraffin and what sounded a very good party (involving 'three Cymric lady navvies' and 18 gallons of ale in a barrel) enlivened Saturday night. Even the mess accounts were in the black! Guy Fawkes day was celebrated (on 6 November) with a major and very effective blast; the previous weekend was notable for a Fox deal involving the acquisition of 5cwt of tinned fruit. Big thinking.

By the end of the year 400 skip loads had been dug, and Deviationists had had people on site on 41 weekends out of 52. In fact, at that rate, another 79 years would have seen the job through!

In 1966, this rate of digging was bettered to one which would give completion in a mere 23 years, but it began (as any fun project should) with a party. On Saturday afternoon, 1 January, a suitably inscribed memorial stone (paid for – causing some controversy – out of mess funds) was 'declared open' at the site of the first ravishment of virgin soil for the Deviation, just 12 months previously. In the evening, 30 partook of a superb dinner in a warm and slightly smoky mess, it being also the debut of the fireplace (with stone mantlepiece which was a six-man lift' and new exterior chimney stack. Previously Dduallt Mess heating had consisted of a biscuit tin balanced on a primus stove under the table round which the volunteers all sat. This occasion was to be the first of many 'first sod' anniversary parties.

In fact during 1966 the Deviationists manned the site every weekend except Christmas. Parties used to arrive late on Friday nights or in the small hours of Saturday morning, park their transport at Tan-y-Bwlch station and push trolleys loaded with baggage and supplies the two miles up the line to the mess. A small party 'representing' the Edinburgh University Officers Training Corps logged a weekend away in Wales in the following stereotyped but informative style. . . .

May w/e 20-24.   E U O T C ffatigue squad.
Reported Mess 0430 hrs., found no work immediately available. Reveille 1100hrs., having carried out quick recce of target before dawn. Paraded 1105hrs. at site 3 with picks, mattocks and shovels generalserviceotherranksfortheuseof. In action 1110hrs. Withdrew 1600hrs. Rations. Counterattacked 1600hrs – rain – mud. Last post 2300hrs, mess orderly absconded.
Sunday re-engaged enemy after short church parade. Weather poor. Ffox keeps complaining. Lunch 1400. Rain. Severe casualties, many skips lost. 2100hrs Ffox AWOL.
Monday squad reduced to three. Trolleys, pump, one

requisitioned QM stores TAN/y/BWLCH. Proceeded site 1. Built track. Dismantled track. Rebuilt track. Proceeded site 2. Desperate attack on rock face . . .
Total skips loaded for week-end: 40 (viz. Approximately 50 tons) Ffestergraph [ie total skips loaded for year to date]: 607.

After the work was finished, the long journey home would begin with a gravity ride on the trolleys back to the car park at Tan-y-Bwlch station.

It was also the case that many Deviationists, who on the whole were students or came from office jobs, found their monthly weekend at Dduallt so physically demanding that they needed no other exercise. Congenial company united in a common purpose, various high jinks, as well as the contrast to their normal life, all played their part in attracting people. As one helped push a trolley on arrival along the deserted railway on the mountainside above Tan-y-Bwlch in the moonlight, London office and flat life would seem part of another existence.

27–29 August, 1966 was another big weekend with 17 bodies – 140 per cent of the mess capacity – at Dduallt. Three slept on the living-room floor and two had a tent outside. A record 108 skips were filled and tipped and the delightful occupation of bog blasting indulged in. Bog blasting is very spectacular and (although you might not think it) very effective: mud slinging on the grand scale, if you like, and accordingly balm to tortured souls. Since mud hurts less than rock if it hits you, bog blasting is far less worrying than rock blasting for the person in charge.

Colonel Campbell, who visited the site on the Monday with his wife and daughter, made a remark which still rings in the annals of the Deviation. When he was asked, as all sightseers in deviation country were, whether the ladies would like to help, he replied, 'I don't think so, they have their husbands already . . .'.

Whether the Deviation girls in fact chased the men or vice versa is almost beside the point, but there were certainly a great many marriages. Others may well have been prevented.

Moragh Walker said she found on more than one occasion that someone who had rather dazzled her in his own environment was pretty ordinary among the Welsh rocks. The small Edinburgh University Group (Devsoc) reported in 1978 that six marriages had taken place between people who had come on their working parties; but, of course, the statistic we should like (but cannot get) would be those who met *first* on the Deviation and subsequently 'lived happily ever after'. In fact a good many of the Deviation 'regulars' got married to one another, succumbing in this way while breathing the rarified air of the Welsh hills. As regards the Junta members, one could use the word 'most', notable exceptions being Gerald Fox and Mike Schumann. Incidentally, 'Junta' is a Spanish word meaning to 'join' or 'congregate', normally used with reference to a governing or legislative clique.

A true Deviationist would naturally view all such matters as Deviation deviationism; the only question he or she would ask would be – did mixed parties help the Cause? To this one must answer an unqualified yes. The men (when not too exhausted by their exertions) liked to show off their endurance, strength and ability to the girls, while there were many tasks in which feminine common sense, carefulness and consideration showed to advantage. One thing must be said here. Communal living quarters and a slightly old-fashioned anti-orgy attitude among the regulars made what used to be called immorality a little difficult. Of course, the energy that might have been expended on such things was needed for the digging. . . . None of this prevented some groups from advertising for volunteers under the slogan 'Have a Dirty Weekend' – one that was only too literally true. Some girls, especially those from the Northern groups preferred to take over the traditional female tasks. But even if this was not so, messing, hygiene and comfort generally was immensely improved by a feminine presence.

The remainder of 1966 and the first few months of 1967 passed steadily. 'Points' – alias 'turnouts', 'switches', 'leads', or 'half-shunts' – appeared so that several rock faces in the 'quarry' at Dduallt station (sites 'o' and ' − 1') could be worked simultaneously. A new chapter opens at this time, however, with mess accommodation tripled and the departure overseas of the Deviation's Founding Father, Gerald Fox.

6

Volunteers' railway

'We are the pilgrims, master; we shall go
Always a little further; it may be
Beyond that last blue mountain barred with snow
Across that angry or that glimmering sea.'
James Elroy Flecker   The Golden Journey to Samarkand

A landmark in this story was passed in the Spring of 1967, when Gerald Fox left Britain for pastures new across the Atlantic. His last recorded visit to Dduallt before leaving was in May and, although he still exercised influence by remote control from the West Coast of America, 6000 miles distant, it was a major event. But no-one is indispensable and the other Junta members quickly adjusted their roles to suit, David Currant (who was not a Cambridge engineer) taking the hot seat as 'front man', while Roger Simons became Project Engineer. One thing that was not adjusted, and was to cause trouble, was the rupture of the unofficial lines which connected Gerald to various members of the FR Board. The official channel of communication via Porthmadog was a trifle overloaded, as we shall see.

A great debt of gratitude is owed by all lovers of the Festiniog Railway to Gerald Fox, who put in an immense amount of time into the Deviation. His work was brilliant and painstaking and his drive incredible; while the man who made no mistakes never made anything, the one he seems best remembered for is a bulk purchase of goat meat at 5p per lb, in an effort to reduce mess expenses. The first group on which it was tried apparently waited until nearly midnight for this material to become chewable and it never did. In the end it served a useful purpose by becoming part of an embankment.

Tunnel Mess opened at Easter 1967; the 12-person mess at Dduallt was fine but its situation precluded any significant expansion, necessary to bring a rate of progress implying a 1989 completion date up to something more reasonable. So the idea was born of a second mess, nearer the upper working sites, on the old FR line by the mouth of the original tunnel. The Company's coffers were empty, so the question of finance was solved by the Junta borrowing money from themselves; in fact, the sum of £500 was provided by Messrs Schumann (£150), Fox (£100), Bradshaw, Currant and Jamieson (£50 each). The Festiniog Railway Society (the FR's supporters' club) agreed to contribute a further £200 while the Festiniog Railway Company agreed to pay off the loan by August 1968.

As a size of group, 12 was considered near the optimum; smaller, and they are less effective; bigger, and they suffer from lack of cohesiveness, and splinter groups form. So the new mess was designed for two parties of 12, bunkrooms at each end with a common messing area in between. The bunks were in tiers of three, 7ft high, but otherwise the arrangements were based on those found so successful at Dduallt. The outside structure was a sectional timber hut 6oft by 2oft, delivered by special train in mid-March and erected in time to provide primitive shelter at Easter. Mike Schumann was responsible for both concept and execution.

When finally fully kitted out – with the help of many handsome gifts – Tunnel Mess had things that grander establishments might envy; its own railway station, for example, and siding, with special trains (opportunities for guests to drive, push or brake themselves) when the public train service was not convenient. In addition to beer, there was real mountain water running from the taps of the Mess, not the recirculated 'purified' stuff townsfolk have to suffer, although it must be said that before one of those engineering conjuring tricks called hydraulic rams were installed, working the large semi-rotary hand pump was a chore some could have done without. Of course the situation was quite incomparable – all this for 50p per night, full board. The porridge alone was, as the *Michelin Guide* would say, 'worth a detour.'

There was never any question of a 'ladies end' and a 'gents end' at Tunnel Mess. Ratio between the sexes varied from being wholly male to 9:1 in favour of female Deviationists, but no trouble was ever recorded. A few (very few) girls protested, plus also one modest young man who thought his mother would not like him to share a room with girls. But he withdrew his objection when he heard that one of them was to be Jen Lemon, the group organiser's wife, who was well-known to Mama. One also notes that a particular lady whose heart was as large as her person was not asked to come again, though it is not clear how much this was due to any straight-laced attitude on the part of those in charge, or to engineering doubts as to whether they had allowed sufficient strength when designing the bunks, for double occupation by hefty and energetic people.

The occupation of the 36 beds available at weekends in the two messes was organised by four geographically arranged group organisers. There was also a secretary who dealt with weekday occupation and outside-organised groups. Behind them was the Mess Secretary herself (sometimes himself) who saw to the accommodation, basic food supply arrangements etc. The details of the arrangements are given in Appendix C 'Lyn Ystradau Deviation – General Information Sheet'.

Two other changes were pending; for the first time the Deviationists were faced with completing a section of line on time for running public trains on a date – Easter 1968 – to which the Company was already committed. In fact, timetables were already at the printers. The work involved concerned the so-called 'Quarry' site at the back of Dduallt Station and a short section of embankment (Site No 1), both needed for the new station layout, so that locomotives could be run round quite long trains.

The second thing in the wind was an impending agreement, hopefully in advance of the Light Railway Order, over the purchase of a long stretch of route 'over the Rubicon', that is across the railway on the other side of Rhoslyn, which would treble the work available.

All these matters really meant a new ball game and it must be recorded that the three parties involved (the Deviation Junta, the Company Board and Allan Garraway, the hard-pressed General Manager at Porthmadog) took a little while to get used to it, as the files bear witness.

The Deviationists to a man cast Allan Garraway as the villain of the piece, and *vice versa*, of course. The scars of their battles still, even now, ache and keep them awake at night. But, objectively speaking, the General Manager of the Festiniog Railway had a duty to give priority to things that directly affected the running of the trains. From his point of view, the cancellation of one train was a major disaster, while a wasted weekend on the 15-year project of the Deviation was not even a flea-bite. He had all the traumas of a major expansion (33 per cent in passenger journeys and 25 per cent in miles of road open as between 1967 and 1968) and of having museum-piece equipment in intensive use; to cope he had only a shoe-string budget and a tiny staff. Of Allan, it should simply be said that he kept his eye on the ball and, as a result, turned – with a little help from his friends – the ruin of 1955 into what is now regarded fairly generally as the premier tourist line of the world. A well-earned MBE came to him in 1979. Echoes of this conflict appear in song – see page 186.

Of course, it is fairly essential that a project should have enemies, for the cohesiveness of the participants is hard to achieve without it. A further one came usefully to hand in the person of one of the farmers through whose land the new line was going to run. This man liked to twist the Deviationists' tails in ways they did not like. But was he beyond his rights in insisting that, for example, people should ask him before performing engineering operations on his land, even if it was only to stand a ladder? In another case, after the FR Company had agreed with him to exchange the new route for the old one, he complained that FR people were pulling down a stone wall, so breaking a sheep barrier, on the land that was going to be his. But why ever should he not? On one occasion a certain group, finding, first, that no one had any matches and, second, that departure time was approaching, went off and left a blast charged with explosive. The account in the log even shows a slight sense of injury that the farmer we are speaking of went off and told the police, though in fact the matter was put right the next day and no danger resulted. But he was suspected of less forgiveable involvement at other times; however, he and the FR are now good friends.

The remit given to the author before writing this book was that the account should tell of the Deviation, warts and all. So here are some, but, after all, they were fairly little warts. In serious matters the Deviationists were very public-spirited. For example, the sites were abandoned for nearly three months, in fact from 26 November, 1967 to 17 February, 1968, with the aim of keeping foot and mouth disease from the hill farms of this part of Wales. Even so, in spite of this curtailment of the working season, the Ffestergraph for 1967 stood at 2279.

This enforced absence was may be also prudent for other reasons. On 19 November an error of judgement caused bad damage to Mr Rhys Davies' vacant Rhoslyn Cottage. Due to a misunderstanding, a blast across the line from the cottage had been too heavily charged. A row of trolleys and skips had been placed to protect the building but: 'in the event six trolleys took to the air, two skips went through the fence of the house, one window was demolished and another holed. A great baulk left its signature on the wooden ply shuttering of a window and there were two major holes in the roof. Many willing hands set to work and in no time at all the tide of loose rock [around the house] receded, brooms were busy on the rooftops and front garden. . . .' Very commendable, but again there was this note of surprise when Mr Rhys Davies 'seemed very irate'. Wouldn't you be? Not content, however, they did it again on 26 February immediately after repairs had been done! But even this did not alienate Mr Davies, because he still allowed the Deviationists on to his land before a legal agreement had been signed. Such are the sheep farmers of North Wales.

After this, events followed thick and fast. The Deviationists' independence ended late on Friday night, 5 April, when the usual trolley movement up from Tan-y-Bwlch became subject to the railway's signalling system and it was necessary to withdraw a single-line staff before proceeding. The Northern Group had, on the previous Sunday, respectfully stood by their skips, shovels at the slope, for inspection by HM Inspector of Railways, Colonel Robertson, RE (retd).

The 'foot and mouth' delay had prevented completion of the loop and when public services began the next day, Saturday 6 April, a spare locomotive (in fact, 103 year old *Prince*) was attached at the rear of each arrival to pilot it back to Tan-y-Bwlch, while the diggers took advantage of drinks available from the buffet car whenever a train stood in the station.

The completion and opening of the loop on 20 May marked the entry of Deviation handiwork into railway service. However (and it is another milestone, inconspicuous but significant) the last stages also marked the first direct outside non-volunteer work for two expert professional rock-men from the Blaenau Ffestiniog slate quarries were employed to do the final trimming of the station cutting's rocky sides. Oddly enough, the experts learnt from the Deviationists how to detonate more than one charge at a time, which they had not done before.

On 27 July came that crossing of the Rubicon and the opening of sites around Rhoslyn's lovely shore. Unlike railways which started by naming their locomotives and later went on to numbers, the Deviation began with numbers, then went to names. Hence Shed Site (which almost at once became Barn Site) and the no doubt well-named Midge Site. Later came Dingle, Rosary, Spooner's Hollow, Dragon, New Moon and Bluebell.

Also in mid-Summer, on 21 July, came the first of the famous 'God Squads' who were to perform such sterling work over the years to come. Organisations such as the Crusaders' Union, the Student Christian Fellowship, the Inter-Schools Christian Fellowship and The Pathfinders, brought parties of young people for a fortnight at a time. Sometimes they brought a portable organ to replace the gap left in the mess furniture by an absent beer barrel. Sometimes, also, on returning, this organ would be arranged on its trolley so that it could be played. Imagine rolling home down the mountain on a gravity train with, up front, organ music giving thanks for all the beauty round about.

Rather than inventing enemies (this being frowned upon by their Trade Union), one thing the God-Squads did to promote cohesiveness among themselves was to publish a daily newspaper. Not perhaps the very highest flight of journalism but still fun was the

MOELWYN EXPRESS and DDUALLT DAILY DIGGER No 5
Industrial Dispute threatens Work Sites:
As is to be expected in these unstable days, industrial strife came to Moelwyn Tunnel Mess yesterday when, owing to appalling working conditions, the National Union of Ffestiniog Deviation Diggers (N.U.F.D.D.) agreed unanimously to stage a half-day token (or train staff) strike. A later snivelling compromise with the grovelling capitalistic management laid down that work would continue until either rain fell again or the water in barn was more than six foot deep.

(Any bias towards the glorious under-paid and down-trodden workers is entirely accidental.)

P.S. It is rumoured that Mr V. Feather is coming to the scene of the dispute on the 17.25 (FX) on Friday.

And now, a final word from the Management.

In spite of Monsoon Maisie visiting Dduallt yesterday work continued almost unceasingly throughout the day. Morale though wasn't the greatest amongst a handful of obstreporous protestors especially after surprise at our enthusiasm was expressed by a rodent blackleg. Rebellion began on two sites at around 11.00 with an almost complete walkout leaving Ganger Pete helpless (as usual).

In spite of the Junta assuming a posture of contempt for railway enthusiasts, the Deviationists by this time even had their own locomotive, although they were not allowed to play with it much. *Alistair*, a Ruston & Hornsby 13hp diesel, was presented to them by a Mr H. A. Bierrum, who had read of their needs in an article written by Dan Wilson which appeared in *Country Life* during November, 1967. Bunny Lewis (of whom much more will be heard) was the only 'Devi' to be passed as a driver while a volunteer.

With the 1968 Ffestergraph standing at 1700 by October, all may have seemed well, but behind the scenes things were simmering. David Currant even felt compelled to write a very fierce and formal letter (in fact a much toned-down version of Mike Schumann's original draft) to Company Chairman Alan Pegler in the following terms:

Alan Pegler Esqr   Observatory Gardens,
                                                      London W.8
Dear Sir,   14th October, 1968
  It is now four years since work started on the construction of the Llyn Ystradau Deviation, and since that time in October 1964, an organisation has been diligently built up to do the job. Originally the work was controlled by Gerald Fox who had gained your confidence during the period of survey of the route and latterly through his dealings at the Public Enquiry. However, by the middle of 1965 Gerald had built up a "Junta" with five other people to help control the construction project. Since Gerald's departure, this Junta had made every effort to nurture a growing organisation in a competent and responsible manner, but has unfortunately had only limited personal contact with the Board.

  After four years and completion of one tenth of the total earth-works, we should have developed a smooth and amicable working relationship between yourselves, ourselves and the General Manager. This, however, is by no means the case. We of the Junta understand that we are working voluntarily on behalf of the Railway Company, and yet we find it virtually impossible to obtain from you, the Company's Board of Directors, the actions and decisions which are essential to the life of the project. It is sometimes extremely difficult to believe that the Deviation is being built with the Company's blessing let alone its guidance. You have given us, to date, no help whatsoever on such matters as the available funds each year or what services from the General Manager we can rely on. As a result of these and other omissions we find it completely impossible to do any detailed planning for the year ahead, and hence to schedule our requirements in materials. We also have reason to believe that the mere fact that we work on an open ended budget, unlike all the other departments of the railway, is the root cause of a certain amount of friction, and the attitude that we are a nebulous and irresponsible group.

During the past year the situation has become particularly bad. If work camps, such as the one held this year, are to be satisfactorily organised for 1969 the details must already be settled in December this year so that the necessary supervisory staff can be recruited and camp programmes finalised for the interested parties. This year's camp would have been a fiasco if Rhys Davies had not been so co-operative in agreeing to allow us on his land before purchase arrangements had been completed. We have been approached by several groups who would like to run work camps on the Deviation next summer. We do not propose to accept or proceed with the organisation of these camps until the Board can satisfy us that purchase arrangements for buying the rest of the land and compliance with the legal aspects of the LRO, with regard to work programme, are in hand and will be completed by the New Year or soon thereafter. We have not yet received from you a single copy of the Light Railway Order, or copies of the drawings upon which the order was based. Since we understand the order not only includes clauses which affect programming of the work, but also features of the actual construction, the situation is little short of comic.

The payment of hire charges for a compressor on such a regular basis as we now find essential, appears to us to be a gross misapplication of funds. The only reason that has been given for not purchasing a compressor to be permanently stationed at Dduallt is that we are not competent to maintain such a machine, and yet the saving that could be made is such that it should be possible to pay someone to give it regular maintenance. As far as our mechanical competence is concerned, we consider that this has been adequately demonstrated by the amount of work we succeeded in extracting from the two ancient relics provided as compressors by the Company. The first of these reached us, supposedly after an overhaul (lasting twelve months), in an unworkable condition.

Above: After sites 1 and 2 have met material is tipped to widen the embankment. Notice the shovelling plate to assist in moving material away from the track. *John Ransom*

Right: Excavation in the cutting at site 3 shortly before the breakthrough into site 4. The barn in the far background, top right, marks the location of Barn site. Note the steel framework for protective covering used when raining. January 1967. *Dan Wilson*

Above: Barn cutting under construction. The pneumatic drill is in use on the top surface in preparation for blasting. Old bull-head rails laid on the ground on their sides are used to form the most temporary section of track nearest to the working face. Nearly all the workers are wearing safety helmets. *FR Civil Engineering Group*

Left: A pause en route while moving a loaded skip to the dumping point; below, Dduallt station as it existed as a temporary terminus for the public train service. Compare this with the earlier view before the new platform was built. The original line to Blaenau Ffestiniog at the lower level disappears towards the bottom left while the new line leading to the spiral curves away centre left. *FR Civil Engineering Group*

We are aware that the Company is permanently short of money, but we feel that most of our problems are caused by lack of determination on the part of the Board to see the Deviation built, an almost total lack of any guiding policy and a failure to make decisions at the appropriate time. In view of the fact that these problems in the main can be settled by discussion, we of the Junta feel that a meeting between full representatives of the Board and ourselves should be held as soon as possible, so that a more satisfactory working agreement can be arranged. We have by no means lost our enthusiasm for this unique project, but we find that our patience as volunteers in the present situation is virtually exhausted.

(signed)

D. A. Currant, Chairman,
For and on behalf of the London Junta,
Festiniog Railway Company,
Civil Engineering Groups.

Copies to:
Messrs. E. J. Routly, W. B. Broadbent, L. J. W. Smith, Viscount Garnock, F. T. Wayne and members of the London Junta.

Your author, having at various times in a long railway career found himself seeing such situations from each of these three positions, feels sympathy with all the parties in this ruction. But sympathy would have been useless, so what did the Board do? Simply this; they rolled out one of the biggest wheels in the whole wide world of full-size railways and appointed him as the Deviation's Man On The Board.

Gerard Francis Gisborne Twistleton-Wickham-Fiennes had had a distinguished railway career. Many people thought he should have been Chairman of British Railways, but alas, a Socialist Minister of Transport did not feel that a classical scholar from Winchester School with a triple-barrelled name was quite in the Labour image. But she could not keep him out of other top jobs on BR, some of which brought him into rather explosive proximity to the man she did appoint. You can read all about it in his vastly entertaining book, *I Tried to Run a Railway*. Gerard Fiennes himself finds the triple-barrelled thing a bit cumbersome and (so he told the FR magazine editor) expects 'Gerry', 'The Guv'nor' or 'Oh, 'im'. Anyway, in spite of a declared feeling that the world's railwaymen are divided into (a) engineers and (b) human beings, he was soon on excellent terms with these strange Wild Men and Gorgeous Girls up in the mountains. He fought valiantly for their cause, first getting them a budget, then a compressor, then seeing that helpful Mr Rhys Davies got compensation for some sheep killed on the line and, most important, supporting a proposal for the Deviationists to have their permanent paid 'Man in Havana' on site. Most of all he inspired better communication between the Deviationists, the Manager and the Board.

The compressor arrived on 30 November at midday. It was a brand new, bright blue, 160 cubic feet per minute job made by Broom Wade. Unbelievable. With the Light Railway Order promulgated it was 'peace in our time' with the Deviation's neighbours. On that same weekend the log records Paul and Moragh Bradshaw, Peter Jamieson and John Grimshaw setting out to meet the farmers concerned and discussing the 1969 programme of work with them. The occasion was referred to as the start of 'Moragh's Friendship Campaign'.

Even so there were still problems, seen (usually) objectively and constructively by Gerald Fox from his earth 6000 miles away, where he was doing a bit of deviation construction on his own with the Bay Area Rapid Transit project around San Francisco. Late in 1969 he wrote:

Supply Systems
    Perennially the most wearing and exasperating problem is that of supply of the materials and services needed to keep the project going. Occasionally it is a large or urgent item; more often it is the routine supply of fuel or explosives with only minor variation week by week. The friction and ill feeling that has arisen is enormous. The Railway Company, in particular the Manager, resent dealing with the transient and many-headed Deviationists and consider any work for them of the lowest priority, and it usually requires a battle or directorial intervention to get anything done.
    The Deviationists are immersed in many more complex matters of recruiting, transport, provisions etc, and fail to see why the

Railway cannot supply the items asked for, if only as appreciation for all they put into the work.

This problem has gone on for many years, and does not change with the changing Deviation personnel. So long as the management holds this attitude I see no likelihood of a major improvement, and so a different approach is needed, as this matter is more tiring than all the other deviation problems, perhaps because it ought not to be happening at all. So it seems to me, our approach to the problem should be adopted to control as much of the supply system as possible direct, to use Tan-y-Bwlch and Colonel Campbell's engine, or *Alistair* for supply, possibly building a road/rail loading ramp in a quiet corner at Tan-y-Bwlch with some sort of hoist (shear-legs as used on canals). This would allow most Deviation supply problems to be solved direct, involving John Harrison (Station Master at Tan-y-Bwlch, known as 'Lord North') but going no further. If a dump for sand, gravel, pipes, coke, oil drums, could be established at Tan-y-Bwlch just below the old goods shed, then it would be within range of Deviation loading parties to come and collect as required outside train hours, and the supplier can deliver by lorry and tip whenever it suits him. Cement and valuable stores should use a part of the old station, as the food supply already does, preferably on an 'A' key, or otherwise accessible to Deviationists.

Obviously the appointment of a permanent man to the Deviation will short circuit some of this, but it would not be useful for me to speculate on this. . . .

You may feel that all these tedious matters are subsidiary to the Great Work, but it is not so. They have been inevitable and even essential on all big engineering projects since long before Stockton & Darlington or, for that matter, Stonehenge and the Pyramids.

In the meantime our Deviationists had discovered the joys of washing off the dust and sweat of battle in the limpid waters of Rhoslyn. Your author, who went to a school which then had a centuries-old tradition of costumeless bathing, accepts without reservation the theory recently propounded by Elaine Morgan in her enchanting book, *The Descent of Woman*, that the human race evolved its naked body and upright posture by spending, millions of years ago, millions of years in the sea. It just feels so right to plunge in *puris naturalibus*. What was lovely in 1967 was a bit trickier in 1968 when public trains – some extra to the timetable – started running! A meticulously observed gentle-persons' agreement to prohibit photography during bathing hours has, alas, prevented us from illustrating the scene. . . .

7
Not quite a volunteers' railway

'. . . It was not a big brass General that came,
But a man in khaki kit who could handle men a bit,
With his bedding labelled Sergeant Whatsisname.'
   Rudyard Kipling   Pharoah and the Sergeant

There was a Deviation milestone on 16 May 1970, because on that day Sergeant David 'Bunny' Lewis, Royal Marines, became its first full-time regular paid pair of hands and, one might add, its first paid tongue.

Almost certainly holding the record for the greatest distance travelled in order to work on the Deviation – mostly from Poole in Dorset – Bunny had been coming up to Ffesters regularly for some time. He had in fact been present at most of the major occasions during the preceding 18 months – and soon enough he was taking charge as a Junta member. Like the Egyptian soldiers to which the quotation at the head of this chapter refers, most of us over 30 had at one time or another had the privilege of receiving instruction from an NCO hailing from an elite section of the British Forces and have benefitted much thereby. Non-deviationists amongst the rest of the British public later had a chance vicariously to experience Bunny in action when he performed in front of the cameras for BBC Television in the 'Go With Noakes' series. The combination of strength and gentleness displayed drew the following tribute from a Barnoldswick schoolmaster and his wife:

> I would like to write a page of his log book to report how satisfying the past fortnight has been for us both. Coming with a

75

group of young people who are in some cases reluctantly undertaking a compulsory fifth year at Secondary School and who have
in almost every case some serious social problem of their own, we
have been impressed with the intelligent and sympathetic handling
of the youngsters by both Bunny and Martin. They have both
stolen the hearts of the girls.

Signed C. Garnett

S. Garnett

Except perhaps for that BBC recording of Bunny saying to
John Noakes 'What . . . AARRE . . . You . . . Doing', no trace
is left of all those words that convinced so many volunteers that
there were only the two ways of doing things, ie, Bunny's Way
and the Wrong Way. Just occasionally a terse comment appears
in writing on the log, indicating that an order from Bunny was
more than just a basis for discussion. His work-sheets for the day,
put out for each group on arrival, were so drawn up that they
leave very little room for any misunderstanding, argument or
manoeuvre. A group leader who reported that some wheel
bearings on a skip were broken, for example, had the remark,
'why didn't he do something about it' recorded against him for
posterity. It is the greatest tribute to Bunny that such unilateral
behaviour has not produced any detectable resentment, either
in reminiscence or in what was recorded at the time. One of
Bunny's slightly disconcerting weaknesses was that he was a
bit apt to say things like 'Ah you lot, go up to the whatsits at
Diddlyalt and fetch the tweaker and while you're about it
bring the thingmybob.' This left all but the experienced
completely bewildered.

One bonus which came from having regular staff on site was
the ambushing, apprehension and, eventually, the conviction
of some youths who had been in the habit of breaking into
Tunnel Mess on Sunday evenings, after volunteer groups had
departed. It was a real 'wait till you see the whites of their eyes
stuff, with the US Cavalry lying in wait until the redskins were
well inside and busy – then lights on and soon the captives
marched across the mountains into custody.

A small debit to put against having a permanent foreman on site was the fact that some people missed the self-reliance that the previous system imposed on them. Mike Schumann, who had by now taken over as project engineer (after some persuasion) from Roger Simons, now married to a non-Deviationiste, said afterwards that the type of volunteer who came was related to the task to be done. Incidentally, Mike was in very much at the beginning, having first come to work on the FR as a volunteer in Easter, 1956, aged 14. He was to see the Deviation through all its vicissitudes to the opening in 1978. To a great extent he has also been the founding father of the project to write this book.

Bunny's duties and various other important matters were defined at a meeting held at Moelwyn Tunnel Mess on 27 June, 1970:

Present: M. Schumann, The Junta, G. F. Fiennes, A. W. G. Garraway.

(1) *Joint Statement of Intent.*

The CEG (Civil Engineering Group) and the FR Co agree as follows:

(a) The CEG's object is to construct a new formation for the FR between Dduallt and Blaenau Festiniog.

(b) The proposals to this end in general should be prepared by the CEG and submitted to the FR Board for approval of route, of the works, of the estimated expenditure and of the rate of progress.

(c) The Director or Directors nominated by the FR Board for liaison with the CEG will be responsible for reporting any substantial deviation from the proposals to the Board.

(d) The FR Co's General Manager will be in control of supply of materials and equipment for the CEG and of transport between the source and the head of steel.

(e) The General Manager will also be responsible for co-ordinating the day-to-day activities of the CEG with those of the operational railway if and when the two activities conflict with each other.

(f) The FR Co and the CEG declare their common intention to complete the new formation as soon as resources permit.

77

(2) *Future expansion of Deviation Activities.*

The Company's policy is that laid down in (1) (f). Accordingly if their claim on the CEGB succeeds fully or substantially a large sum will be available in 1971 and succeeding years which will radically expedite the Deviation. If the claim fails, the Company will allocate sums from their current resources which they hope will considerably increase their present contribution. The figure of an increase of 50 per cent was mentioned and not thought unreasonable, given the present level of traffic.

(3) *Progress of West Shore Route.*

The survey is complete. Drawings are being prepared for submission to the CEGB. The CEG will prepare broad estimates, based if possible on a 'budget' quotation from a contractor.

(4) *Role of the Company's first permanent employee on the Deviation.*

The General Manager will draw up a job specification for Mr Lewis which will take account of the following principles:

(a) Mr Lewis' prime responsibility is to encourage and facilitate the progress of the Deviation.

(b) In pursuit of this end he will agree the programme of work with Mr Schumann or his deputy.

(c) He will be responsible for the delivery of material and supplies as required.

(d) He will ensure that the parties have sites and work available for them.

(e) He will from time to time inspect the progress of the work.

(f) He will co-ordinate the work on the Deviation with that of the railway if and when any conflict of interest arises.

(g) He will – see below – act as Deputy shot-firer to Colonel Campbell.

(h) He will keep the General Manager informed.

(i) As a second duty he will encourage the development and happiness of the volunteer effort on the operational railway.

There was some discussion about the proportion of time which Mr Lewis could devote to (i). The Company's director considered that after a little while it should be around 50 per cent and gained little support for this figure. The meeting agreed that they would review experience in September.

(5) *Shot Firing.*

A report was received that Colonel Campbell was firstly having difficulty in renewing his explosives licence and secondly not wishing to undertake shot firing as frequently as in the past.

The meeting agreed that subject to Col Campbell's agreement and training Mr Lewis should become his deputy; being appointed by the General Manager as the Company's shot-firer.

The question whether the Company should take out an explosives licence was deferred for Col Campbell's views.

In the meantime any hiatus in licences should be covered by a local contractor.

During July and August, 1970, 'permanent way' was laid on the Deviation as far as Rhoslyn Bridge. This familiar and rather misleading term is used to distinguish between the 'temporary' track (*very* temporary in the case of the Deviationists) and track used for running proper trains. Again, there was an occasion worth recording when, on 22 August, a special passenger train gingerly picked its way on to the spiral for the first time. The main reason for doing this work was to provide access to Rhoslyn Bridge for works trains conveying beams, concrete etc, when making the permanent deck. In fact this 'permanent way' did not remain long enough to enter public service.

A performance by a London Group on 14–15 November 1970, of 103 skips loaded by hand seems to have been the first century for a normal two-day weekend. Subsequent efforts far surpassed this but they had the assistance of mechanical excavation. The Ffestergraph that year ended up at 2720.

Even so, by early 1971 there was a move for 'Dragon' site to be called 'Drag-On' site. The work of completing Rhoslyn Bridge occupied much of the volunteer effort, but as greatly valued was the project to construct a septic tank at Tunnel Mess. Was there any connection between this and prune-eating contests between the God-Squads and the Deviationists? Incidentally, birthdays in the mess were often celebrated with candles in porridge, and on festive occasions there were such traditional mess games as crossing the room from end to end against the clock without putting foot to floor. These served a useful purpose when the food cupboard overturned and accordingly got a much-needed cleaning out! Outdoors, Bunny soon put a stop to mud-fights, but tea-tray tobogganing on heather and grass (occasionally on snow) continued.

Linda, with Alan Garraway at the regulator, first crossed Rhoslyn Bridge with a special train carrying most of the FR staff, on 1 July 1971. In August came another major advance, with the acquisition of a second-hand Massey-Ferguson 244 crawler-loader tractor complete with back-actor excavator. With cab removed it could travel by narrow-gauge train. Together with two dumpers also acquired round about this time, this equipment improved production per man-day by a factor of at least 15. The Massey was not too happy loading broken rock, but fortunately there was some boulder clay (very hard to deal with by hand) to be dug at this stage, particularly on Bluebell site. The presence of competition incited some Deviationists to incautious speed. On 31 August, stitches were needed in one feminine leg and one masculine hand, one of the very few occasions on which the work led to hospital treatment. By the end of September, except for two small gaps, the Deviation grade was complete from Dduallt to the place known as Two Trees, where the West Shore and East Shore routes diverged.

It fell out very nicely, therefore, that all was in order to begin on the West Shore route and this took place with ceremony on 15 October 1971, just before the compensation award was to be announced. Heath Golding, the CEGB's Power Station Manager, came along to see how his employers' money (if they lost) was to be spent.

The main survey of the West Shore Route was carried out during the summer of 1970. It just so happened that two students from the North-East London Polytechnic, Dick Davies and Nick Nicholson (Nick was later to marry Deviationiste Caroline Fryer, Gerald Fox's step-sister), were able to do it as part of their course work. One result was the end of Imperial units on the Deviation; new all-metric country began at a new zero point by 'Two Trees' site. As for actual construction, the point at which work was to begin was at the dam referred to in Chapter 1, which was originally built to provide waterpower for hauling FR trains up the incline which preceded the original tunnel. Track level was 15ft below the crest of this dam and, to start forming the necessary gap, a ceremonial 'first stone' was removed by Mr Golding. The gold-painted spade was not appropriate here; but it was more than made up for by golden toe-caps on the site foreman's protective boots. Some conundrums for Festiniog archaeologists arose over the dismantling of the dam; these were produced by the findings of smooth faces which indicated successive enlargements. As the dam was dismantled, water flowed out around the workers. During heavy rain work was abandoned for fear of them being washed away. In spite of all of these distractions, the Ffestergraph for 1971 stood at 4467.

The Massey was moved to the dam site at 'first sod' weekend in 1972. Some will no doubt wonder how these winter working parties kept warm in a none-too-well insulated hut on a none-too-sheltered site in the mountains. Coke-burning stoves were favoured, partly because solid fuel is more companionable and partly because users got a vivid impression of how much they were using. Coke was also cheaper anyway. Occasionally the mess stove's limitations were discovered, as witness the site log for 15–16 January, where it was reported that a diet of stale bread, over-age sandwiches, various articles of clothing (including two right shoes) some diesel fuel and a little coke gave the stove violent indigestion.

A great event on 4 March was Bunny's marriage to Deviationiste Jane Ayres. Work went on, however, and the log rather charmingly reported that the whole Deviation scene was beautified by a blanket of snow. 'Perhaps this was nature's tribute to an event which was taking place many miles to the South'. The remark is perhaps a reflection of the strangeness of the area. For example, the old FR found that Dduallt station masters tended either to go mad or become great poets; herds of wild goats roam the vicinity and unexplained noises in the night were unhesitatingly attributed to the supernatural.

When the happy couple returned, there was a surprise extra wedding present from the Company – a locomotive called *Jane*. Both Janes were to continue giving sterling service to the Cause for a long time. Actually this locomotive was not new to the Deviation; it was an existing Simplex machine which had been overhauled, improved, re-painted and given a name.

Chris Chitty writes:

Keith Tyler and I ran a working week, known as the Tyler-Chitty week, in successive summers. Bunny would allow us one day off and so Keith and I decided to climb Moelwyn Bach. It was one of those still, hot, clear days and every sound in the Vale of Ffestiniog could be heard by us. At the time the council were widening the main road and an excavator could clearly be heard about two miles away with its bucket crashing and banging as it loaded rocks into lorries. Keith turned to me and said, 'You know, Jane must be having a good effect on Bunny already, even from here, I can hear him doing the washing-up'.

It was the custom on the Tyler-Chitty week that we would take Bunny and Jane out for a meal one evening in the week. Bunny would always show one up on occasions like this. We were in the Royal Sportsman Hotel in Porthmadog one evening and Bunny, having already attracted the attention of other diners by his behavior, banged the handles of his knife and fork on the table and said, 'Ah! dins,' to the amazement of the demure and petite waitress arriving with the meal.

Incidentally, I got to know Bunny's ways early on; during the summer of 1969 he got me to paint some notices directing the tourists to use the stile and not climb over the gate. This having been done I could not find any white spirit to clean my brushes so I decided to clean them in diesel fuel which I obtained from the fuel filter on our then brand-new compressor. This created an air-lock in the system and it would not start, so I decided to bleed the fuel system and in my enthusiasm sheared off one of the bleed bolts. I was dismissed to Boston Lodge to get the parts repaired by a furious Bunny and he referred to me thereafter as 'The Twit'. This name stuck for many years. [Even in correspondence with Bunny during the writing of this book. Author]

These last years before leaving Dduallt were a happy period. The organisation was working well, new plant was coming in at a rate enough to enjoy but not too much so that it took over. A particularly amazing project was one to buy a Smalley Excavator with Green Shield stamps, amazing not only that anyone should have had the temerity to think of it, but also because it was successful beyond anyone's dreams.

The appeal went out in the issue of the Festiniog Railway Magazine for Winter 1972–3. The 5900 members of the FR Society were asked to produce 6700 filled books of stamps. A certain Mr Youell saw this appeal and it produced in him the sort of sympathy one might feel for someone setting out to cross the Atlantic single-handed in a rowing boat; he suggested that his plant-hire firm should buy the Smalley and rent it out free to the Company for as long as they wanted it. The money raised by the stamp appeal was used for many other smaller but essential items; of the Smalley itself, more later. Meanwhile, the Ffestergraph for 1972 stood at 3466.

On 17 March 1973 more than 500lb of high explosive taught the rock in Barn Cutting some manners; the intention was both to improve the eventual alignment as well as to produce fill needed for the final layout of Dduallt Station. The large cutting was almost filled up by the blast and seven skips worked the run on real permanent way between Barn and the station. *Jane* (the locomotive) broke her chain in the excitement; even so 93 skips were filled.

'They'll never believe this one' records the log for the following week when 'ten bodies (9m, 1f) plus Bunny, Jane, Martin Duncan (the Deviation's second paid hand) and the digger cleared 252 skips in four days – weather brilliant – literally – throughout, and this is perhaps the easiest week I can remember in Ffesters.' Nine weeks and 1150 skip-loads later there was a way through. The one-day record was broken – Bristol with 165. Some clearing up remained but it is recorded that the Permanent Way Department began work on 24 June. A far cry from the early days (in fact, an output of this size represented almost the average of the first two years' work), especially if you consider that several other sites were worked during this period. Virtue was its own reward, however, because a large conducted tour on the occasion of the Society's Annual General Meeting will remember little of the quiet site they found, but much of 'a Cheltenham lady surprised sunbathing in bra and panties.'

Now only the Mess at Colonel Campbell's remained to connect the Deviationists with Dduallt and even this was shortly to go. The reason was partly that Col Campbell wished to have it back and partly that work was beginning higher up and a pair of cottages in Tan-y-Grisiau were now more convenient even if not as nice. Volunteers also had the use of part of a house belonging to Mike Schumann and Paul and Moragh Bradshaw. The last party stayed at Bottom Mess in the late summer and the fittings were finally removed to Tan-y-Grisiau on 17–18 November. 10,000 bed-nights had been provided at Dduallt since 1965.

With 'first sod' weekend (the first in January) always big-time on the Deviation, Christmas working parties were not as regular. But, this Christmas Eve of 1973, we note Chris Chitty leading his Northern Group troops out to serenade Tan-y-Bwlch Station House, Mr and Mrs Johnson's cottage at Coed-y-Bleddiau (another rail-only abode) and finally at the Colonel's. The log records: 'probably the first time for 300 years that carol singers had arrived at Dduallt. We were lavishly entertained by the Campbells and all staggered back up the line to recover for Christmas Day.'

The Northern Groups had a tradition of socialising; after a hard day's work they thought nothing of the three-mile walk from Tunnel Mess to 'The Grapes' at Maentwrog, where they would sing the place down with the locals. Other groups tended to work on the Deviation only but the Northern sometimes liked to join in and work in other departments on the operating railway. These Christmas 'do's' were a case in point; on Christmas Day itself they would fill one ceremonial skip, sing more carols at the Power Station (to the amazement and amusement of the staff in the control room) and have Christmas lunch with red and white wine in one of the slate mines – provided the cork-screw had not been forgotten. A slap-up traditional turkey dinner in the Mess would follow in the evening.

The carols that those Deviationists sung that Christmas of 1973 were also, perhaps, a lament for a lost Eden and great days that had passed for ever. The way ahead had been signed clear for all to see in September, when the first major civil engineering contract on the Deviation – for drilling Tunnel North cutting – had been let. Although Deviationist ego was satisfied when the contractor found the granite harder and the peat softer than his rig was accustomed to, nevertheless it was apparent that the future was largely with specialists, big corporations, and, above all, paid staff.

Furthermore, instead of woods and pastures round a lake, the new working areas involved harsh uplands where eagles soared. *Per ardua ad astra* in fact and with a certain appropriateness a distinguished airman, Air Vice-Marshall Sir Ben Ball, KBE, was invited on to the FR Board to replace Gerard Fiennes, who had resigned in order to give himself more time for local affairs in his home town of Aldeburgh.

It was now the exception rather than the rule that excavation was done in traditional 'Armstrong' fashion. The brand-new Smalley Model 360/15 Mk II presented by Sterling Plant Hire Ltd of Coventry arrived on 20 August 1973, and from then on, apart from breakdowns, two major mechanical diggers and two members of the permanent staff to operate them (or instruct in their use) were normally there whenever digging parties were on site. Something of the regret felt for the old days must have inspired the *Moelwyn Express And Daily Ffestergraph* to run a special edition in memory of the de-thronement of the mattock . . .

THE MOELWYN EXPRESS AND DAILY FFESTERGRAPH

SOUVENIR EDITION
TO MARK 763 HAPPY YEARS OF MATTOCKING

In the year of Grace, one thousand two hundred and ten, an English gentleman and part time inventor, walked abroad on a tour of the principality of Gwynydd. His name Charles Henry Mattock, later to assume the Welsh title of Iarll Mattock and founded the town of Portmattock, named after him, however I digress. Quite by chance he happened upon a little known town of Ffestiniog which at the time had little industry except for the chicken mines.

Mattock being a man whose curiosity always got the better of him, naturally wished to see over the mines. After being shown over one by the foreman a bearded giant, Dafydd Lewis, who was known to all the miners as 'Cwningen', (the rabbit) he was amazed to see how primitive the methods of excavation were. The only tools in use at the time were long iron bars used to prize out the chickens, known as chicken bars (since chicken mining died out in Wales, they have been known as crow bars).

Mattock being an inventor, decided to provide a better tool for the job, so he invented, you've guessed, the pickaxe! This tool was an initial success, and mines who employed this tool were able to undercut their competitors and gain valuable contracts in the giblets market.

Flushed by success Mattock improved on his design and invented the Mattock. Rumours flared around Ffestiniog, mining shares boomed on the rock exchange at Stryd Mur (Wall Street) and whole fortunes were sunk in chicken mining. All the mines sank huge sums in the purchase of mattocks.

Disaster struck, the mattock was untried and when the miners swung a mattock above their heads to strike a blow at the rock, the head slid down the handle and jammed the miner's fingers!

The result was a national chicken mine strike, the mines went bust and most people lost their fortunes in the Stryd Mur crash which followed.

Mattock, in disgrace, fled the country, scavenging hordes roamed the countryside attacking unwary travellers with mattocks.

It was now no longer safe to walk about after dark without a good lantern, due to the thousands of discarded mattocks strewn about. An un-whitting person could easily step on the broad end of

86

Above: The first of the permanent beams of Rhoslyn bridge about to be lowered on to the pier cappings. A little repositioning will be needed so that the near end is clear of the temporary sleeper packings. After the tie bars are removed lowering will be completed by the two Tir-for pull-lift devices. *FR Civil Engineering Group*

Right: Double Fairlie *Merddyn Emrys* approaches Campbells siding with the special train conveying the concrete beams for Rhoslyn bridge on the spiral at Dduallt. *FR Civil Engineering Group*

Above: Rhoslyn bridge; the site before construction began, June 1967. *M. Luck*

Below: The end result; a trial train headed by *Blanche* crosses the new Rhoslyn bridge while *Merddyn Emrys* brings the service train into Dduallt station underneath. *FR Civil Engineering Group*

a mattock, hidden by the undergrowth causing the handle to fly up, hitting him right in the 'mattocks'! Yes 'mattocks' had become a dirty word, and with the continuing violence the mattock became political dynamite. Elections in the area were fought and lost on this issue alone.

The violence, however, gradually diminished and only one incident was ever recorded. A group of malcontents, dressed as local shepherds, successfully besieged a small mattock factory near Portmattock. Clearing out the tons of old tea leaves from the Grott, they dumped it all in the sea, hence the Cob. This incident became known as the Boston Lodge Tea Party.

So, over the centuries, the mattock drifted into obscurity along with the chicken mines, the huge tips of feathers having long since blown away. In later years the slate mines came and went, obscuring the disused remains of the chicken mines with their enormous grey tips and erazing them from the hillsides and the memory of man forever. So mattocks and chicken mines remained, until in 1965 a bright young man from Cambridge University started building a railway . . . with mattocks! Who knows where this madness will end?

Some of the allusions in this elegant piece of nonsense become clearer if you have handy a copy of Elizabeth Beazley's book about William Madocks, Porthmadog and the building of the famous 'Cob', called *Madocks and the Wonder of Wales*. In later years – even to this day – this so-called Anniversary of the Invention of the Mattock is celebrated by the old hands of Northern Group; sometimes just an evening in a pub but on occasion excursions by train as far afield as Thurso for John o' Groats. But it was modern plant that lifted the 1973 Ffestergraph count to a record 5163 skip-loads.

8

Bridge builders of Rhoslyn

'. . . his own kind would judge him by his bridge, as
that stood or fell. He went over it in his head, plate
by plate, span by span, brick by brick, estimating
and recalculating, lest there should be any mistake;
and through the long hours and through the flights of
formulae that danced and wheeled before him a
cold fear would come to pinch his heart. His side of
the sum was beyond question; but what man knew
Mother Ganges' arithmetic?'

Rudyard Kipling   The Day's Work

Bridge building is one of the most satisfying activities known
to mankind and accordingly the deviationists looked forward
to the three new bridges together with ten or so culverts and
sheep creeps, all to be built on the original deviation line. Of
the bridges, first came the Rhoslyn Bridge carrying the new
line over the old at Dduallt. Because there was no road access
and also because its completion occurred in the Deviation's
'shoe-string' days, the methods used owed something to that
great engineer *manqué*, W. Heath Robinson. Of the other
bridges, those across the dam and approach road on the East
Shore Route were eventually to be replaced by four almost
identical buried bridges carrying the line over the power
station penstocks or pipe lines; but with these the Deviationists
had little to do – they were part of the contract work supervised
by Sir Alfred McAlpine (Northern) Ltd. On the other hand the
West Shore Route did include a wide-span bridge over the
Cwmorthin River just short of Tan-y-Grisiau station. This was
to be largely a Deviationist effort, but aided by every sort of
modern plant from concrete vibrators to 100-ton cranes.

RHOSLYN BRIDGE
& Cei-a'r-Bont

Fig 7   Sketch of the original proposal for Rhoslyn bridge. *Dan Wilson*

The original proposal for Rhoslyn Bridge involved a stone arch of 'traditional' design. In the event the rock on which the bridge foundations were to be built was found to be fissured and accordingly considered unsuitable for the sideways thrust of an arch. Some difficulty in finding craftsmen capable of the rather skilled work of constructing masonry arches was also anticipated.

Therefore a simple three-span bridge of concrete beams sitting on reinforced concrete columns (two to each pier) was substituted. One advantage of this design was that it provided without extra cost the two cattle creeps, one on each side, which had been specified in the Light Railway Order.

The making of these piers was undertaken as a 'crash' job at New Year 1969. The task (as well as the reason for doing it in such a hurry) was evocatively described by John Grimshaw (shortly to leave for Uganda) in issue No 2 of the more serious version of *Moelwyn Express*:

> Four pairs of columns and capping beams to Rhoslyn Spiral Bridge were finished on 14 January, 1969.
>
> For some on their next visit to Festiniog, this sudden appearance on the skyline of four stark groups of concrete columns may come as something of a shock, and they should realise the events leading up to this structure. Imagine Barn site towards the end of the Summer, now three-quarters of the way through, its tip edging up to the old cutting and the rest of the rock destined to widen site three embankment. We needed a temporary bridge or a permanent one, or a combination. This work had to be finished by the beginning of the passenger season in March. Now also imagine the finished line. Either folk could pass up it, never noticing what was new and what was old, so faithfully had the builders reproduced the techniques and feeling of the nineteenth century quarrymen. Or coming to Dduallt they would have to say 'this is new'. There are no halfway houses. And the first we cannot build – no one could, there is not that kind of skill left in Wales today. But how to design in the mountains. After a long time of continuous change we realised that our designs must resolve themselves around the criteria of minimum labour and minimum materials. For we have not got anything like enough of the former (particularly skilled) and

we have not got the plant to handle quantities of the latter. Now this is exciting because Ffesters is a small place and the scale is such that given the right sort of vision and ideas, the engineers could build unique and beautiful structures. It might be a gate or water overshoot but we must be sensitive to that solution that is so right that we can look at it and say – just say nothing because it looks and is right. As to the building, the date was fixed for early January so that there could be labour during the school holidays, so that the cold prevented the concrete setting too fast, and to be finished before the new season. Roger (Simons) worked and re-worked the design so that the Consultants, Livesey and Henderson could sign them by mid-December. The final design is pairs of 18in diameter columns joined by a capping beam, this carrying precast concrete beams over three 16ft 6in spans at some future date. Mike had a hectic time locating materials and equipment, and Mr Creamer had to empty Wales during Christmas to find what we needed in the way of plant. And the foundations had been dug and drilled when eight from Westminster School, Chris, Ros, Bunny and I appeared at First Sod Day. After all the festivities we stayed on and worked. The problem was that NO float days were left in the programme, and it was January. No clear picture remains of the building, only isolated flashes of memory. . . .

– of trollying down Moelwyn with lanterns in the morning
– of rain, more rain, dripping macs and cold, slippery scaffolding
– of John Harrison fighting diesel and tobacco fumes in the winch engine
– of concrete and more concrete
– of Dougal the scaffolder with red woollen cap and spanners in his belt
– of the Colonel fretting ill in bed in the Manor, longing to be up on the mountain
– of more concrete, concrete being winched up through the birdcage of scaffolding, dribbling grout on Hugh and John below
– of Bunny's language deteriorating to the barrack-room floor as the week progressed and he kept us laughing – laughing so much that we had to rope Dave to the Tubes.
– of the fantastic food produced by Ros
– of beautiful clear skies with horizons tipped up over Manod
– of complete freedom to work as hard and as long as one wanted away from the petty regulations on site and knowing that we were all in it together
– of the Manager and his hound on their frequent visits

– of concrete and yet more concrete and the hurrying to have all
the scaffolding and shutters ready
– of floodlights far into the night with this little world, this little
patch of brightness isolated so high on Moelwyn
– of warm bags in the mess and the alarum clock ringing us awake
It is a patchy record of a time we enjoyed and our thanks go to
all who make it possible and our apologies to those who would have
liked to be there but did not know, or were ·unable to come.'

The cast of this drama were:

Members of a Junta	John Grimshaw and
	Roger Simons
A Designer of Bridges	Roger Simons
A Works Foreman	Bunny Lewis
A Manager	Allan Garraway
A Manager's hound	Del
A Maker of Heavenly Meals	Rosalind Neuburger
A Winchman and Station Master	John Harrison
A Carpenter and Chronicler	John Grimshaw

Chorus of – concreters, scaffolders, steel-fixers, etc, Nick
Sanderson, Nick Hodgson, Dave Somervell, Chris
Chitty, Dougal Campbell, Simon Crame, Hugh
Watkins.

But, ladies and gentlemen, does it or does it not sound like the
writing of a man in love? Having already made sure of her
cooking, John Grimshaw was later to marry Rosalind.
Incidentally, 'Rosary' site was named after her and a girl
called Hilary Forrester.

What was very much a non-love-story nearly marred this
play, raising a problem of what might be called the 'non-
problem' type. Clearances between moving trains and Welsh
rocks on the old part of the Festiniog Railway were governed by
the consideration that actual physical contact should be
avoided, while for new work the Ministry insisted that a wide
clearance each side of 1ft 6in, was needed. The Deviationist
design for the Rhoslyn bridge piers, however, very reasonably
gave clearance to moving trains no better than the narrow

cutting in which they were situated. They perhaps had made a mistake in thinking that rules were for the governance of fools but the guidance of wise men.

The absurd position had, in fact, been reached where there was a threat that the new piers would have to be re-sited – Allan Garraway had to take the difficult decision to allow work to continue. But the threat was not finally extinguished until Gerard Fiennes in the nick of time both suggested and carried home the view that, if the cutting face was artificially restored where it had been cut away to build the piers, then honour and the law (but not logic or common sense) would be satisfied. It was a narrow squeak from action being taken that might have led to complete withdrawal of further voluntary work on the Deviation. But this little bit of nonsense was good training for other absurdities of bureaucracy to be met with further up the line.

As intended, then, the piers supported temporary girders and track over which spoil from Barn site could be run down to complete embankments lower down. The final concrete beam deck had to wait for nearly two years.

What are called pre-stressed concrete beams are fairly standard for bridge-building nowadays. The 5-metre standard Dow-Mac T-beams for Rhoslyn were no exception, being bought 'off-the-shelf' (or nearly so) and delivered to Minfford Yard by road. One snag as compared to steel beams, say, is that one must be very careful how and where pre-stressed beams are slung or lifted. An attempt to lift by a sling at the centre would mean an immediate goodbye to any useful further existence for that particular beam. All this was kept carefully in mind while the beams were transhipped from road to rail at Minfford and unloaded at Dduallt without mishap in November.

The periodical *Concrete Quarterly* sent a writer to observe on the weekend in question, 4 January 1971, but his account says practically nothing about the little bridge or its erection. He was instead more stunned by a site of amazing beauty which 'offers a pint of beer on arrival at 2 am' which (then) had only one paid employee, and where very great things had been done – the concrete bridge being only a minor part of them.

In the event the beams were slung from pairs of rails supported by trolleys at each end; the trolleys ran on to the bridge over some specially strengthened temporary track, so arranged that each beam could be lowered between the rails (temporary tie-bars having been removed) into place by 'Tir-for' pull-and-hold devices. The gauge was widened slightly to 2ft 0½in to allow the 600mm wide beams to pass between the rails. The temporary track and the position of sleepers supporting it above the piers, were adjusted between 'drops' to suit the position of the next beam to be lowered. Beams in line on three successive spans formed each 'drop'. The whole operation went without a hitch and was a very enjoyable occasion, happily recorded for us by the camera. The lifting system used nothing but equipment already available.

This happy result was due less to luck than very careful forethought and planning. The erection scheme was shown on a comprehensive drawing prepared by Gordon Kennedy, a specialist on the erection of pre-cast concrete structures with Holland, Hannen & Cubitt who, through that mysterious Ffestiniog magic, plus an appeal in the magazine, just happened to write in to Mike Schumann on 13 October 1970:

> . . . As a member of the Festiniog Railway Society for about six years who has been unable, hitherto, to contribute anything practical to the Railway, it would give me much pleasure to have a busman's holiday on the project. . . .

For laying the filler concrete between the stalks of the pre-cast T-beams, another concrete expert from John Laing & Co, called Tom Merrick (an Oxford man this time, would you believe) gave a hand, specifying an additive called Poyzolin which can have the effect of retarding the setting of the concrete by several hours. Hence it was possible to have high quality ready-mixed concrete delivered – water added to the mix only at the last moment – to Tan-y-Bwlch station and run from there to Dduallt by train, without danger of spoiling. Ready-mixed concrete had also been used for the making of the columns two years earlier, but in the absence of such advanced techniques the last truck loads to arrive tended to have already set, needing to be hacked out with mattocks, and so wasted.

The scheme was as follows:

PROGRAMME FOR SATURDAY, MARCH 20th, 1971

08.30 5 'Hudson' wagons to be ready at Tan-y-Bwlch (3 wagons to be held there in reserve).

09.00 Readymix concrete wagon to discharge $4\frac{1}{2}$ cubic yards of concrete into wagons. 3 sample cubes to be taken.

09.15 Depart for Dduallt.

09.30 Arrive at Dduallt. Locomotive to push two wagons at a time round spiral to the bridge, where they are to be manhandled singly on to the deck and discharged from one side, stockpiling concrete over crosshead beams.

11.00 Locomotive to leave Dduallt with at least three empty wagons.
As many sections of jubilee track as possible to be lifted from the bridge, and spreading, compacting and tamping of concrete to continue.

11.15 Second train to be assembled at Tan-y-Bwlch, comprising of six 'Hudson' wagons and locomotive. Wagons to be lined with polythene sheeting.

11.30 Readymix concrete wagon to discharge $5\frac{1}{4}$ cubic yards of concrete into wagons. 3 sample cubes to be taken.

11.45 Depart for Dduallt.

12.00 Repeat procedure for first train.

15.00 Locomotive and wagons to be clear of main line and loop in Dduallt Station.

15.20 Arrival of 14.30 train from Portmadoc.

Again, careful forethought ensured success.

For later working parties there were the water-proofing, parapet walls, handrails and other details, after which Rhoslyn Bridge was handed over to the permanent way department for tracklaying. As has been mentioned, the first passenger train crossed the bridge on 1 July, 1971. Since the line had not then been passed by HM Railway Inspectorate, fare-paying passengers were not carried either then or for several years.

The Railway Inspectorate had insisted that a firm of consulting engineers should oversee the design work. In this case Donald Halstead and Partners – who had taken over from Livesey and Henderson – felt that inadequate provision had been made to resist side-pressure due to high winds, in combination with centrifugal force and 'nosing' of locomotives. Accordingly, some side-bracing columns inclined at 45deg were added to the outer piers (Nos 1 and 4) during a series of weekends in late 1973 and early 1974. Entries in the log, which refers to these additions by various names (side supports, bracing struts, transverse columns, etc) seem to imply a certain doubt among the volunteers as to the necessity for this work.

The little under-bridges – culverts or sheep creeps are perhaps a more usual description – all had head walls, wing walls, etc and so were an opportunity for people to learn and enjoy the gentle art of building with random stonework. Francis Turner was the Deviationist who became their master stone-waller. Concrete pipes formed the basis of most of them, and the manipulation of these into place was good clean fun; they are heavy and intractable objects and with the least inattention are liable to roll away to the bottom of the valley. It was traditional for builders to crawl through the culverts they had made, a little disconcerting in cases where they were only 24in in diameter and quite long. The construction of these structures usually preceded the tipping of embankments over them. When the sheep creep at Gelliwiog was being built, a group of tourists were persuaded that it was for North Sea gas!

9

Organisation people

'. . . the table was covered with the intimidating
remains of some kind of a meal in which porridge
seemed to have played the chief part.'
Stella Gibbons   Cold Comfort Farm

Napoleon is supposed to have made the famous remark about
an army marching on its stomach, but, as regards food on the
Deviation, eight years of experience, much of it no doubt
traumatic were behind Mess Secretary Jenefer Lemon's
instructions – see page 178. Napoleon's armies did not, however,
have to pay for their own food and here the Deviationists'
welfare was looked after by such heroic means as removing the
labels from tinned fruit to ensure random consumption
amongst the expensive and cheap kinds – it happened in-
advertently when a consignment was left out in the rain and
Mess Secretaries were quick to take the hint – so the Mess
charge, originally 10s (50p) per night, was in fact kept constant
in real terms over the years. In 1979 it was £1.50.

Mike Schumann's mother produced a recipe for Stew à la
Deviation, suitable for complete strangers to the kitchen and
designed to be cooked in Tunnel Mess' formidable pressure
cooker. Yellowed now after years of exposure on the wall
behind the stove, it reads:

DDUALT & TAN-Y-GRISIAU JUNC.
RAILWAY CONSTRUCTION GROUP

Recipe for Standard Mark I Stew

Ingrediants [sic] for twelve hungry mouths
   5lbs steak and kidney chopped up
   2lbs carrots

1lb onions
1 tin of tomatoes
1 tin butter beans
½ pint beer
plain flour
salt, pepper, assorted herbs
Bisto or Oxo
Method.

Put the beer in the pressure cooker together with the tomatoes, butter beans and cleaned and sliced carrots. Start gently to heat. Fry cleaned and diced onions in fat until golden brown and then add into pressure cooker. Roll meat in flour with salt and pepper added and then fry in fat until partially cooked on all sides. Place in pressure cooker. Dissolve Oxo cube in small quantity of water (less than ¼ pint) and together with herbs add into pressure cooker. Stir contents.

Fix lid on pressure cooker and set safety valve to notch 3. Place on high gas and wait till whistle blows then set to notch 4 and adjust gas to keep pressure constant (20 psi). Cook for ten minutes and then carefully remove lid. Eat.

Bunny Lewis' idea of the ultimate in stew was to place everything he could lay hands on, including baked beans and prunes, into a pressure cooker and curry it into the ground. After a hard day's work on site it was delicious and even people who didn't like curry ate it.

Northern Group were responsible for the 'Action Butty' which consisted of two slices of bread, cheese, pickles, tomatoes and Unox Spam, which was referred to as 'Yonks'. The London Groups referred to Corned Beef as 'Corned Dog' and Pork Luncheon Meat as 'Pressed Pussy'.

A malicious rumour was put about by the Northern Group at one stage claiming that Mike Schumann was ordering fruit cake without cherries in as opposed to cake with cherries as it was a farthing a ton cheaper.

At times there was intense inter-group rivalry; the Northern Group always reckoned that they filled bigger and better skip loads than the London groups. Whether true or not, on one occasion they took this ideal to extremes and continued to fill an already full side tipper by building up a tower of rock way above the skip. It was a foolish thing to do because when they tipped the groaning wagon (it must have had at least 3 tons in it), the wagon, frame and even the track tipped with it and they spent the rest of the afternoon retrieving the skip (top and bottom) from the base of Dragon embankment.

The fun aspects of the Deviation are the ones that have been emphasised so far in this book, but, in order that some could have fun, others had to beaver away steadily on the chores in the back-room. The fat files of London working party organiser and Deviation Secretary Christopher Noel, for example, tell something of the story. One day in 1973, for example, we find him replying very disarmingly to Mrs Phyllis Gordon-Spencer of The Duke of Edinburgh's Award Scheme, who was 'considerably concerned to receive a letter from the parents of a girl who recently volunteered to help with the Festiniog Railway Project, that no separate sleeping accommodation is apparently made for young men and young women. . . .'

2.5.1972

Dear Mrs Gordon-Spencer,

Thank you for your letter of the 10th April; I apologise for not having replied sooner.

It is unfortunate that we never made this particular point known at the outset. Although we always aim to tell individuals, it did not occur to me to tell you, any more than it apparently occurred to you to ask!

I gather Deirdre Lewis has explained the position to you, and I have now prepared a statement confirming the various points which she mentioned. I am enclosing 14 copies for circulation to your various organisers.

Our project supervisor remembers the girls concerned and tells me that they had known about the project from a personal friend who has worked on it. When asked, they had apparently expressed no objection to the accommodation but said they were leaving as one girl was suffering from migraine. At the time they were there the mess was occupied by Post Office personnel engaged in your Award Scheme together with their own very responsible leader, and a family party with children.

Please don't think I am attempting to avoid the issue, but I feel obliged to report the incident as it was explained to me.

Yours sincerely

(signed) Christopher Noel

His files contain copies of many letters in reply to individual enquiries; none are in stereotyped form, but couched in the terms most appropriate to the individual concerned. There was always a little touch of gallantry for the girls; listen to him replying to Hilary Gawthorne after she had declined to take on the job of mess secretary, on the grounds of her forthcoming marriage to her 'man of the moment . . .'.

Dear Hilary,

Many thanks for your letter and many congratulations.

I sometimes wonder if there will be any single girls left by the time I'm in the mood for making decisions! [but there were – and quite soon. Author.]

Obviously, I thoroughly understand that you can't take on any more commitments. The easiest way of returning the hat is to drop it in here next time you are passing, and I'll let it be known that the owner can retrieve it from me.

With best wishes,

(signed) Chris

When it came to sending out supplies of the recruiting leaflets, 'Building Back to Blaenau', to Youth and Voluntary Organisations (of whom one discovers when delving into Deviation documents that there seem to be an inordinate number), again it was not just a question of a circular letter, but an individual one tailored specially to the contact or organisation concerned.

All this was really the tip of a huge iceberg. Advertisements inserted in national and local newspapers were set out in such terms as:

WEEKEND PIONEERS WANTED

Railway Building N. Wales – Ring 734 8765 or evg. 937 2674

So, all the complications of travel arrangements were done over the telephone. Sometimes the scale of complexity dealt with comes to light when the odd written communication is found to have survived, as here:

21-6-71
Dear Mr. Noel,
  Re the transport arrangements for Mark Pedlingham and myself for the working party on 17th and 18th July. If you travel on the M1, as I assume you will, it would be more convenient to meet you at the Toddington service area (No. 2 between Junction 11 for Dunstable and Luton, and 12 for Bedford) rather than at Hendon. Leaving Hendon at 19.15 I think you should be at Toddington at about 19.55 pm. So, if you are agreeable, we should like to be picked up from the downside (Northbound) car park at the service area at 19.55 pm on Friday 16th July. We shall be in one of our fathers' cars, either a white Rover 2000 AOU 907C or a gold Cortina 1600E DPC 18J.
  If this arrangement is unsuitable could you please write to reach me by Friday June 25th or, alternatively, after that date to Mark Pedlingham at 22, Melrose Avenue, Cove, Farnborough, Hants., as I shall not be available again until June 11th.
                              Yours sincerely,
                              (signed) Chris York

The telephone was, however, the normal instrument of communication. Mike Vila (London 'A' Group Organiser, from 1973 to 1977), who definitely preferred the local newspapers of outer London for his advertisements, mentioned the importance of follow-up. When a working-party date was approaching, regular volunteers were asked as a matter of course whether they were coming as usual, while those who had only been once or twice were rung up and invited personally by the group organiser to come again. Naturally it was borne in mind that a working-party with two many tyros was unsatisfactory.

The delivery of some 20,000 person-days of work per year (worth perhaps £250,000 at present day rates) did not just

103

happen; in fact it meant a great deal of work and it is not surprising that Group Organisers tended not to do a stint of too many years. Among those who 'bore the burden and heat of the day' in this role, but who receive no mention elsewhere in this account may be mentioned: Alan Pietrie, John Bayes, Mike Merchant and Andy McWhirter of the London Groups; Patrick Marks, Sheila Ross, Roger Moore, Mary Small and Tim Oakley of various western groups; Melvin Stafford, David Yates, Chris Byrne of Northern Group.

It was lucky, perhaps, that by the beginning of 1974 such an excellent organisation for feeding volunteers both at and to the Deviation had been built up, because, in spite of what has been said in the last chapter, a huge task for the volunteer force lay ahead; 8000 skip loads of material had to be taken from Tunnel South cutting, for example, before boring the tunnel could start. Moreover, Mike and Bunny were already homing on to a fixed date – Autumn 1975 – for this to happen, so therefore the work had to be done to a tight schedule. As disaster followed disaster at Tunnel South the schedule got tighter and tighter.

Both the Massey and the Smalley were the heavy pieces in the Battle of Tunnel South and perhaps a word is in order regarding their respective capabilities. The Massey is really just a tractor with a bucket for shovelling at the front and a small digging attachment at the rear. On the other hand, the Smalley is a proper excavator which, by an ingenious principle, operates without any driven wheels or tracks. The absence of any separate means of movement makes the machine a very good bargain – very important when you set out to save Green Shield Stamps. But at the same time it is so arranged that it can move itself around and about by sticking the bucket into the ground and pulling, shoving or slewing as appropriate. It could be said that both machines were perhaps a little small for the very heavy work they were to be given – and this led to less than 100 per cent availability. A motorised skip-hauler called *Monster* provided through the enterprise of the North

Above: The Grand Bog Railway No 2; the Massey-Ferguson excavator is loading while deviationists at the far end are tipping and spreading excavated material. Tunnel mess is just to their right.
Below: The interior of Tunnel mess with some of the deviationists. Left to right are Mike Schumann, Martin Duncan, Stuart Crystall, Bunny Lewis and, far right, Michael Vila. *FR Civil Engineering Group*

Above: A Royal visit to the head of steel near Tunnel South site; behind Her Royal Highness Princess Margaret are seen Ffestiniog Railway chairman, John Routly, and Mike Schumann. *FR Civil Engineering Group*
Below: The complex temporary track work at Tunnel South working site installed for construction to ensure a smooth flow of loaded wagons away from the site and empties on hand for further loading. *FR Civil Engineering Group*

Staffordshire group of the Society, was particularly prone to mechanical failure.

The material to be disposed of was divided between peat, usually far too soft to be handled conveniently and rock, usually far too hard. Both the Grand Bog Railway and the Lower Bog Railway (1974) Ltd (Bog Railways Nos 1 and 2 respectively) were laid at various times to run the peat away; they were steep, high speed, temperamental lines which vied with one another for the world's record for the greatest number of derailments per yard per day. Skips on the Bog Railways were controlled by placing a bar through the back wheels, thus locking them. Ideas of speeding things up by doing without the bar didn't work – Mike Schumann and Chris Chitty riding postillion on the initial run had to 'abandon skip' at 15 mph.

Because of the great depth, the rock was taken out in two layers, with the Deviation's (but not the FR's) first funicular railway, used for taking skips safely between the upper (temporary) floor and the level outside. It was worked by an air-driven winch. Drilling was to be by contract but no less than three drilling rigs had to be laboriously brought on to the site before one was discovered which was not found wanting. Tunnel North cutting, which was smaller anyway, was not excavated to its full depth in 'pre-Ffunnel' days (Ffunnel= Ffestiniog Tunnel, Yes?). Since the gradient ran down to the site of the tunnel mouth, and no drainage was possible until the tunnel was bored, a lake was the result. At Tunnel South a more temporary lake formed during the removal of the peat. Inevitably the pool was marked with a sign – which, believe it or not, took in many casual sightseers – reading:

BLAENAU NAVIGATION
SITE OF LOCK NO 57
WRYSGAN FLIGHT

In spite of the hard work – and it was hard work, too, even with all that machinery, just because the loaded skips came so thick and fast – the Deviationists had time to think of other things. Mysterious entries like 'MD and AC were seen walking hand in hand over the hills' appeared in the log the same weekend that a rather reluctantly gallant entry to the effect that a girl (in fact the 'Ros' of 'Rosary') had had to be let off rock shifting because she was expecting, also appeared. The ladies got their own back now and again; one notes a biting piece of sarcasm in a feminine hand describing how the lads had carelessly derailed a loaded skip just before quitting time: 'and the dear, good, clever, kind, strong, handsome men got it back on in only just over an hour. . . .' Anyway, Martin Duncan and Alison Cooper announced their engagement in the site record book on 16 November 1974. Their marriage followed in December. Martin still works for the Festiniog Railway Co.

Other notable events of 1974 included the pegging out of the new Tan-y-Grisiau station site on 9 February and a special passenger train to Gelliwiog on 25 August. On 26 August, a site record was claimed when six persons managed only one skip in three days. Even so, the Ffestergraph for 1974 totalled 6166.

By the beginning of 1975, the tenth anniversary of 'first sod', there were still 4000 skip-loads to be extracted from Tunnel South, but in spite of that, confidence was such that work had started across the valley at Tan-y-Grisiau at Christmas. A 2ft diameter culvert, 110ft long, over there must have been a very alarming crawl, assuming that the Deviation tradition was maintained in this case.

An important milestone was 17 May, 1975, because on that day the first significant length of the Deviation entered public service. It took the form of a peculiar little one-car diesel train which shuttled to and fro between Dduallt and Gelliwiog, where passengers were not given the opportunity to alight.

A Royal Train ran right up to head of steel by Tunnel South on 25 July, carrying HRH Princess Margaret on a visit of inspection. It is thought to be the first ever to run on the FR. *Blanche* did the honours, Lord Linley travelling on the footplate from Minffordd to Tan-y-Bwlch. At Tunnel South, Michael

Schumann, Ronald Lester and David Lewis (it was not a moment for nick-names) were presented to Her Royal Highness. All went well, the weather was good, the Princess gracious and happy, and all enjoyed themselves. The railway got a well overdue tidy-up.

Some words of explanation of matters so far left obscure are due here. David Lewis (so the *Festiniog Railway Magazine* says and it would be unlike them to make it up) got his nickname rather surprisingly by, as a young sea soldier, having a passion for setting things on fire. 'Firebugs', he was called and this became 'Bugs Bunny' and thence 'Bunny'. Incidentally, the Cambridge connection of early Junta members was maintained in his case, even if town rather than gown.

You may also have noticed that, like a railway kind of 'grandmother's footsteps' game, if the Deviationists turned their backs for a moment, permanent way seemed to run up behind and touch them on the shoulder. The agency behind this apparently supernatural happening is made up of those other volunteers of whose very existence the Deviationists were not supposed to be aware.

When Gerald Fox received permission to start work on the Deviation, it was a condition that he must not poach the volunteers who helped on the operating railway as part of the Festiniog Railway Society's effort, but instead recruit quite separately. This proviso was faithfully kept; hence 'us' and 'them' and 'never the twain shall meet'.

The laying of permanent way, however, was a matter for the operating railway. Therefore, Supervisor Ron Lester (who was shortly to leave the FR service) and Ganger Norman Gurley laid out the sleepers, screwed down and fished up the rails, ballasted, lined and tamped the track, with the aid of gangs of these invisible men. Exceptionally, during the panic to get things ready for the Royal visit, a 'God-squad' group proved themselves capable platelayers. Incidentally, Norman Gurley is co-editor of the Magazine with Dan Wilson previously mentioned.

A nice present came to hand at this time; Mr Eifon Williams of Blaenau Ffestiniog (a member of the family firm which owns the Oakley Quarries) had long promised to do something to aid the Cause. An opportunity came in the Summer of 1975 when the Williams dumpers and excavator plus other plant moved in to carve out the long shelf on the mountainside leading from near the dam northwards toward the Power Station.

The last effort before all eyes became diverted on to the tunnel construction, was the laying out of a spoil-handling complex and marshalling yard on the area at Tunnel South formed by material dug out of the cutting. In the event all was ready for the miners.

With so many professionals lending a hand, a 1975 Ffestergraph would not be meaningful; the work done in the last part of the year included some carried out with loaned plant on the section north of the tunnel.

10

New Moelwyn Tunnel

'My responsibility is too great to allow of my
retaining for one moment from any feeling of
personal regard, the services of any one who may
appear to me to be inefficient from any cause whatever and consequently it is an understood thing that
all under me are subject to immediate dismissal at
my pleasure you will perceive that I state all these
conditions in strong and perhaps harsh language
and that in substance thay are exactly what I stated
to you.'
Isambard Kingdom Brunel. Letter to William
Glennie on appointment as Resident Engineer for
Box Tunnel, 1836.

The boring of tunnels, whether for railways, mining or
anything else, is a rather fraught and hazardous operation.
Mother Earth resents such liberties being taken with her person
and is liable to take reprisals on those responsible. But, leaving
all that aside, in any civil engineering project – and it applies
as much to building a garden hut as to the Menai Bridge – one
has a choice. Either one finds a hut builder or bridge builder
and asks him for a price, or one gets equipped with hut-building
or bridge-building equipment and does it oneself. The New
Moelwyn Tunnel was no exception, although the hazards of
tunnelling weighted the job very heavily against do-it-yourself.

In 1971 five civil engineering firms with tunnelling
experience were asked to tender for a 274-metre New Moelwyn
Tunnel. Only two submitted quotations and these were
respectively for £122,546 and £56,024.85. Civil engineer
John Dalison had put forward the idea of a 50ft deep cutting

instead of a tunnel, his calculations showing that the cutting might be 10 per cent cheaper. The tenders for a cutting were £149,684 and £57,653, and showed (insofar as they showed anything) that the contractors thought the balance lay marginally the other way. Incidentally, the high tenders were probably a polite way of saying that the tenderer did not want the job. But costings of 1971 were totally irrelevant to prices prevailing in 1975.

Now it just so happened (amazing, isn't it?) that two tunnel-driving experts were trying to force their services on the Festiniog. Bob le Marchant had been around when Rhoslyn Bridge was being built and suggested then that he would like to help if there was any question of a do-it-yourself tunnel. Peter Hughes heard about the Deviation and wrote to Mike Schumann to suggest that do-it-yourself – with a little expert assistance – was both feasible and desirable. Peter had a friend and colleague called Robin Daniels who was enough of a 'Steam Christian' to come along too. All three men were Cornish and all had plied their trade not only in one of Cornwall's few remaining tin mines, South Crofty, but also around the world. Bob was also a graduate of the famous Camborne School of Mines, as well as being a qualified mine captain.

Mike Schumann had the responsibility of evaluating the do-it-yourself idea, setting out a balance sheet on which one item was conspicuous by its absence – his own fee for the heavy load he personally would have to bear in a do-it-yourself situation. A man who has successfully obtained heavy engineering plant with Green Shield stamps finds it less difficult than an ordinary mortal to persuade others into original courses of action; incidentally it is very doubtful whether more than a handful of railway tunnels in Britain (two exceptions were possibly the others on the FR) had ever previously been built by men directly employed. The estimated cost for what was now a 284-metre tunnel, 4·5m high and 3·5m wide was £50,000 as against over £120,000 by contract.

The first thing that Mike had to do was to go to market for a DIY Tunnellers Kit, following advice given by correspondence from the miners. This included, mainly, rather stronger, newer and more plentiful versions of items the Deviation was already using. A hired compressor with four times the capacity of the Deviation's own one plus some really good rock drills complete with air leg support for horizontal drilling. There were lots of skips, pipe, track and drilling steels; sectional buildings began to appear plus a complete but second-hand screening plant to sort out some 6000 skip-loads of stone into useful and other sizes. There was a standard steel explosive store complete with lightning conductor. No more keeping the stuff in the Mess loo, as had happened before Bunny's time!

Special for the tunnelling was one of the FR's most costly things ever, the £5,800 air-driven self-propelled Atlas-Copco Mine Loader or Mucker. This device (the first compressed-air powered motive power to run on FR metals, and almost certainly the last) was designed to load rock from the floor of a tunnel or mine adit into its shovel. When full the shovel could be lifted over the loader to deposit the spoil into a skip standing on the track immediately behind. It was designed to swivel each side of its own track to clear a passage up to 10ft wide. You could call it an 'Over the Shoulder Boulder Thrower'! Also needed for the tunnelling was a battery-driven locomotive. By a happy chance the FR's own track gauge was virtually mining's standard gauge, so both these items could be obtained off the shelf. The locomotive was in fact second-hand.

The following document was drawn up as the basis of an agreement with the miners. It was later modified so that the back-up forces working outside the tunnel could share in the bonus, but the principles remained valid. In the event, also, they preferred Saturdays off, when the shops were open.

NEW MOELWYN TUNNEL

Project Definition
    The project will encompass the following works –

1. Boring of the main tunnel to stated profile and making safe from all loose rocks.
2. Pressure grouting or rock-bolting any unstable zones.
3. Enlarging the cross-section where a refuge is required by up to a maximum of 300mm all round.
4. Culling a drainage channel on either side of the floor.
5. Removing all loose rock from the floor of the tunnel.

Definition of Responsibility

Those items listed under Project Definition will be the responsibility of the miners, three in number, in their entirety.

The procurement of plant prior to the contract and its delivery to site will be the responsibility of the Project Engineer and Site Agent.

The responsibility for setting up the plant at site will be shared 50/50 between the miners and the Site Agent once the miners have arrived on site.

The responsibility for bringing supplies to site during the course of the project will be the Site Agent's except where two people are insufficient to do the job and no Deviation volunteers are available to help.

The skips, loaded with tunnel spoil will be delivered by the miners to a point on Tunnel South Embankment and the empty wagons collected therefrom. One miner will be available to help empty the skips.

Tunnel Specification

1. The tunnel is to be built true to line and level. No rocks may encroach within the void generated by passing the cross-section along the centre line.
2. The walls and roof are to be cleared of all loose rocks.
3. The floor of the tunnel is to be cleared of all loose rocks and debris.
4. The drainage ditches are to be fully excavated.

Construction Time

For the purpose of calculating the construction time one month should be allowed for setting up the site and one and a half months for clearing up on completion of the main bore.

Remuneration

The miners' normal working week will be considered to be 6

days at 10 hours; Sunday will not normally be worked and in addition two other days per month will not be worked.

Payment will be based on a fixed weekly wage, a progress payment and a terminal bonus. The sum set aside for terminal bonus will be divided into four portions, one for each of the three miners and one for the fourth man.

(Signed) M. A. SCHUMANN   5.6.75

The first task was to drive a pilot heading to full width but only 8ft high and, in boring this, the miners' plan was to aim at 8ft forward progress daily. The work cycle was:

1. to drill
2. to blast
3. to await dispersal of fumes and dust
4. to muck out
5. to extend and adjust the track for the next stint.

The most convenient way was for (3) to happen while they were in bed, so the day really began around 7 am with (4) the mucking out. A typical cycle involved the drilling of 48 2·5m long holes and the loading of between 40 and 50 skips.

Two differences from excavation in the open air were notable. First, the pattern of drilling in the tunnel included a very closely spaced pattern of electrically-fired charges at the centre of the bore, which were blown fractionally earlier than the others to create the space needed to give proper fragmentation when the rest detonated. Second, of course, there was the long dispersal time for fumes and dust in a blind hole; for this reason, any delay which prevented a blast being set off in the evening as normal, was liable to preclude completely any work on the following day.

By the end of August, as planned, all was ready for battle to commence. The miners were on site, equipment was ready and the black flag of Cornwall was flying proudly from tunnel HQ. Formal approval of the Wales Tourist Board's grant of £50,000 for the new railway works was one of the last prerequisites before work could commence, which it did early that month.

The miners, perfectionists to a man, expressed dissatisfaction with the work done but from this distance the rate of progress seems magical. Difficulties were encountered with fissured rock in the first few yards, but once properly inside the mountain they went great guns, the halfway stage being reached around the end of the year. Veins of gold in the debris caused great excitement at one moment, but the FR Guardian Angel for once said she wasn't that soft – in fact, as you've no doubt guessed, it turned out to be 'fool's gold', ie iron pyrites and arsenopyrite.

A slip in Tunnel South cutting stopped work underground for three weeks while the debris was cleared; a dubious retaining wall on the incline above fortunately came down too. Peter Hughes suffered a foot injury which put him off work for a few days (if he had not been wearing safety boots the injury would have been serious indeed). These and a few lesser pieces of nausea made it a bit of a rush to break through at Tunnel North, in front of BBC cameras, as planned, early on Saturday 1 May 1976. In fact four shifts were worked in two days, following which all concerned departed for a week's holiday.

No mention has been made of the hard and exacting work that went on outside the tunnel to ensure, basically, that every time the mine loader filled a skip, an empty one was ready in the adjacent spur to take its place. The shunting of empties forward and loaded skips backward went on continuously, using the battery locomotive. Spurs were laid in the main tunnel line at 40m intervals to pass empties by loaded cars; they were situated in recesses which would in due course become the tunnel refuges.

It had been hoped that sufficient track ballast would be produced by the screens to make a worthwhile contribution to permanent way expenses. In the event this was less than expected because of the irregularity of the supply. The second-hand screens and conveyors were not wholly reliable, having a tendency to become blocked or to jam when any abnormal shapes or sizes appeared. Much manual effort (of the kind traditionally reserved for convicts) was needed to break up on a grid of rails called the 'grizzly' any rocks produced from the tunnel which were too large for the system to cope with. Bunny Lewis, Martin Duncan, Norman Gurley and newcomer David Payne took the brunt of all this effort. One chore, mornings and evenings, was to tow the electric locomotive back from and down to Tan-y-Bwlch for charging. Yes, you have guessed, under nationalisation, people who make electricity may not sell it! Deviationist weekend working parties played their part in generally rehabilitating tools and equipment, relaying and repairing track as well as disposing of accumulated debris.

As regards the actual boring, now only the 'easy' bit remained, that is the enlargement of the bore to its full height. The through draught now cleared fumes and dust quickly; moreover, a miner could stand on the debris brought down by one blast while he drilled for the next. However, true to the cussed traditions of tunnelling, the 'easy' part of the work was amazingly painful, difficult and long drawn out.

During the euphoria of May 1976, could anyone have imagined that the tunnel would not only not be anything like ready for the booked start of the train service at Easter 1977, but its non-completion would still delay the final opening of the Deviation in 1978? In fact, at that time, there was serious talk of frills like having paved concrete permanent way in the tunnel.

On 17 August 1976, tipped off by an anonymous 'well-wisher' (would it have been the same one who moved the pegs that first weekend 11½ years before?), the Health and Safety at Work Inspectorate sent down two Factory Inspectors. When these gentlemen arrived, the miners had been engaged in enlarging the south end of the tunnel from inside, working on the tricky operation of dealing with the unstable rock that existed here near the entrance. They had been working from inside because there they were protected by rock which they themselves had strengthened and made safe. However, non-miners would naturally feel safer in the open air, although vulnerable there to any rock on the face above that might get dislodged, and this is perhaps what confused the Government men and made them insist (at the threat of a 'stop order') that what the miners regarded as the more dangerous and tedious course of action be followed. Not entirely without protest, for it was their own lives that were at stake and no one else's, the miners complied and with every precaution, enlarged the entrance section from outside; but there was a considerable delay and a great deal of acrimony. Afterwards, Mike Schumann received a telephoned apology from the Inspectors' superiors for their actions.

The most serious problem, however, was that of the tunnel lining. Mike Schumann had reasonably taken the view, when drawing up a specification for the New Moelwyn Tunnel, that since the Old Moelwyn Tunnel nearby had stood with its natural rock bore intact for over a century without being lined, the new one would not need lining either. One could see quite undisturbed the sooty coating left on the old roof by steam locomotives which had ceased to pass 30 years ago. On the other hand, the new tunnel seems to have been driven through a more veiny type of rock; the fact that high explosive was used instead of gunpowder may have made a difference, while a quite different view of engineering safety in such matters now prevailed in the world. It was necessary in any case for Messrs Henderson, Hughes and Busby, successors to Livesey & Henderson, consulting railway engineers, to approve the tunnel as, without their certificate, HM Railway Inspectorate would not allow the line to open. In the event the consultants were not satisfied with the comprehensive programme of barring-down loose rocks and rock-bolting which had been undertaken and insisted on a lining of sprayed-on concrete. They said:

January 1977
REPORT ON INSPECTION OF EXTENSION OF RAILWAY LINE FOR THE LLYN YSTRAUDAU DEVIATION PROJECT OF THE FESTINIOG RAILWAY
The inspection of approximately 1,500 metres of formation of the

west shore route from the point of divergence between east and west shore routes was carried out on 8 January 1977 by the following personnel –

      F. G. Hollis   – Senior Railway Engineer
      P. G. Jordan   – Geologist
      I. J. Middlemiss – Tunnel Engineer

THE TUNNEL

The tunnel which is about 284m in length has been driven through a pinkish-grey medium grained very strong granite which is fairly uniform throughout the length. The rock is generally fresh, though penetratively weathered along joints and more deeply altered adjacent to mineralised veins which are usually fairly conspicuous owing to the presence of white quartz. The weathering appears to be largely related to the present ground surface and is most pronounced in the portal areas.

It is understood that the present mining staff intend carrying out a thorough scaling throughout the tunnel and as this is done additional 2m long resin bolted untensioned rock bolts will be installed where considered advisable, with particular attention being paid to the areas in the roof, of flat slabs which at present only have one or two bolts. *It is confirmed* that this is a *prime requisite*.

In addition it is recommended that the tunnel should be lined throughout with 4in [100mm] of shotcrete built up in layers with light mesh between the layers. This should be placed from a level of about 6ft [1·80m] above invert [ie bottom] up and over the crown. It is important that the mesh should be closely pinned everywhere to the earlier layer of shotcrete, even though this will involve careful cutting and shaping, in view of the inevitably irregular rock surface. Drain holes should be provided through the shotcrete against any possible build up of hydrostatic head.

There are several places where the rock is degraded by alteration close to veins and fissures, and these places should be treated with a total thickness of 6in [150mm] of shotcrete taken from invert across the crown to invert.

These lengths were identified in the tunnel with the assistance of one of the mining team and it must be stressed that the chainages are approximate. In addition, it is possible that after scaling, one or two other short lengths may appear and merit similar treatment.

The Portals

Both portals should be provided with designed concrete retaining structures extended into the tunnel for such a distance that the heavily jointed and more penetratively weathered rock would be *completely supported*. These will extend about 10m in along the centre line from the present portal face at the north end and about 7m in at the south. Each structure should incorporate a head wall above the tunnel and the wing walls to provide protection from weathering of the overburden.

It is understood that the slopes above and adjacent to the portal are to be tidied up, including trimming back of the overburden, removing all loose rock, and improving the surface drainage. Particular attention must be paid in this respect to trimming back and making safe the existing sloping rock face (in closely fractured rock) on the west side of the south portal.

TUNNEL APPROACH CUTTINGS

The tunnel approach cuttings are in rock with overlying clay. It is understood that the rock cuttings are to be scaled clear of all loose debris and the overlying clay cuttings to be battered at an incline not exceeding 2 in 3 and provided with protective vegetation. (signed) HENDERSON, HUGHES AND BUSBY.

It just so happened that John Routly had been at Cambridge with Arthur Henderson and it is pleasant to record with gratitude that, over the years, it was very rare for the FR to receive an account. This applied both to Livesey & Henderson as well as to their successors Henderson, Hughes & Busby.

In respect of the tunnel all concerned took a heavy load of responsibility. Mike Schumann writes:

The building of the tunnel took much more effort than we had ever planned for. Those working on the project drove themselves on relentlessly and the continuous strain showed at times in frayed tempers and near nervous breakdowns. For myself, I felt largely helpless being so far away, and yet responsible for having started something which could and should not be stopped. It seemed to me touch and go sometimes whether a particular section would be finished before there was some human calamity. In building the Deviation we have often seemed to travel on a knife edge between success and total disaster due to over-stretching our resources both human and material. The tunnel construction was the only situation which actually gave me nightmares. I have great admiration for those who saw the tunnel construction through for I believe I could not have done what they did myself.

As regards the lining of the tunnel, even if Mike Schumann had been a little over-sanguine in thinking that lining would not be needed, at least he erred in good company. Brunel made exactly the same mistake as regards Box Tunnel on the Great Western Railway.

It was later agreed that this lining of sprayed-on concrete need only be applied to the most critical areas for the 1977 summer train service, but there was still a serious delay in implementing the printed timetable, which showed the tunnel as due to open on 3 April. The story of the concrete spraying was, in fact, quite a saga; one which, however, will be left until the next chapter. In 1977, the following dates give the way things turned out:

Event	Date	Notes	Locomotive
First through train	7 Feb.	PW Works train	*Moel Hebog*
First steam train	28 May	Test train. Clearances found wanting.	*Mountaineer*
First inspection	29 May	for Major Olver, RE	*Mountaineer*
First (special) passenger train	15 June	for BBC with special permission	*Merddin Emrys*
Official opening	25 June	for invited guests	*Merddin Emrys*
Second inspection	6-7 July	for Major Olver, RE	*Mountaineer*
First revenue-earning train	8 July	15.15 ex-Porthmadog	*Merddin Emrys*

On 25 June, the official opening train stood at Tunnel South cutting for speeches by Chairman John Routly and the Plaid Cymru MP for Merioneth, Mr Dafydd Ellis Thomas, who

afterwards cut the white tape and declared the New Moelwyn Tunnel open. 'Such a charming, modest and sincere man, so unlike a politician', said someone. Ninety-three year old Sir Clough Williams-Ellis was noticeably amongst the more active and adventurous members of the party wandering amongst the construction debris, but alas it was his last visit to the FR, for he died the following year. Charles Spooner was still alive when he was a boy.

Before the trains ran, the miners had drilled 5600 holes, filling them with over 13 tons of special ICI Tunnel Gelignite. About 5000 cubic yards of material had been removed from the tunnel. Eight-hundred rock-bolts had been fixed with resin cement into drilled holes, making up the total distance drilled to over 10 miles. As completed, the length between portals came out as 270m.

Considerable regret was felt when Bob le Marchant resigned in May; among other things, he had felt slighted in that a report he had submitted 12 months previously, which made almost identical recommendations in respect of the tunnel lining to those of the consultants, had been ignored. He had prophesied the problems over clearances and 'shot-creting' as well. In his new occupation of turning South Devon's derelict mining enterprises into profitable tourist attractions under the *aegis* of Dartington Hall, hopefully he may draw some comfort from having been right when everyone else was wrong. At the time, of course, he might well have heeded the late President Kennedy's dictum, 'don't get mad, get even.'

The other miners left by agreement in due course; Peter Hughes is back at South Crofty and is understood to be 'captain' of the 340-*fathom* level (a fathom is *six* feet). Robin and Sue Daniels (Sue is his Deviationist wife) are also in Cornwall, prospecting with a view to reopening certain tin mines, now that ores with a very low percentage of tin can be worked viably.

The completion of the tunnel was an opportunity for Bunny and Jane to fulfil the next stage of their life plan; they left the railway in 1977 as a first step on the road to keeping their own

Above: The bare face of the south portal of the new Moelwyn tunnel with material for temporary track extension being carried in. Note the compressed air main on the left of the bore. *FR Civil Engineering Group*
Below: Approaching the power station: using a bucket suitable for the removal of light topsoil a tracked excavator keeps two large dumpers busy. *FR Civil Engineering Group*

Above: Ready-mixed concrete brought by lorry to the nearest point of road/rail access at the north end of the new Moelwyn tunnel was loaded into the rail-mounted drum seen here which transported the concrete for the last mile to the tunnel. Here the concrete for spraying the walls and roof of the new tunnel was transferred from rail to a spraying hopper and delivery pipe in Tunnel North cutting. *Ffestiniog Railway*

Left: A train emerges from the north portal of the new Moelwyn tunnel on 15 July 1977. The portal is seen here with a bare concrete surface and was later faced with stone. *Dan Wilson*

pub. If ever a reader should find himself in Essex, the Goat and Boot Inn, East Hill, Colchester (unless they have moved on) is well worth a detour – in your author's case more than one special journey. David Payne took over Bunny's duties.

11

Fort Lewis

'What's a thousand dollars? Mere chicken feed. A poultry matter.'

Groucho Marx   from the film *Cocoa-nuts*

As has previously been mentioned, three conditions had been laid down before the Festiniog Railway was allowed to pass close behind the Tan-y-Grisiau power station and its reception centre. First, that the construction work there should be done by a reputable contractor on the CEGB approved list; second, that he should work without the use of high explosive; third, that the work should be completed within nine months.

Coupled with all this came the announcement in September 1975 of the Government's Job Creation Scheme to assist in reducing unemployment. Under these arrangements any non-profit-making enterprise could take on men to carry out approved work; a grant of 110 per cent of the cost of their wages would then be payable. This would allow a margin for the cost of tools and materials which the new employees would use.

Rumour has it that the Festiniog Railway Chairman was knocking on doors in Whitehall that very day, only to find that the civil servants concerned then only knew as much as they had read in their newspapers. Soon enough, however, the FR found itself at the front of the queue as the worthiest of worthy causes. An arrangement to employ a group of 9 (later 12) men on the Deviation was quickly reached and the positions filled; work began in January. The main task for some time was Culvert No 2 at the old dam; being 8ft wide by 6ft high and 60ft long, there was plenty to keep the new team occupied.

It was now a question of making a bigger deal for the main job behind the power station, but negotiations went aground on the snag that all the approved contractors of the CEGB, strange to relate, worked only (hopefully) for profit. Therefore they could not employ Job Creation men. The whole idea might have stayed on the rocks were it not for another remarkable 'just so happened'.

When Alan Pegler went west, literally and figuratively, in the USA with *Flying Scotsman* during 1970, the man who rescued her and brought her back to Britain was Bill MacAlpine. Now it is surely giving away no secrets to say that MacAlpine was a name that appeared on the CEGB approved list. Thus the way was made clear for the negotiation of a remarkable contract, believed to be unprecedented, whereby MacAlpines (in fact, Sir Alfred MacAlpine (Northern) Ltd) provided a Site Engineer and Site Foreman, as well as supervising and taking responsibility for the work done. At the same time the Festiniog Railway provided (through Job Creation) the labour force of 42 men at its peak, as well as plant and materials.

Of course, the 10 per cent surcharge allowed on the cost of labour was nowhere near enough to cover the cost of plant, materials and the management contract. In fact, the estimated cost of the work from opposite the Southern boundary of the power station compound to Tan-y-Grisiau Station was £247,000, made up as follows:

Management cost	£ 20,000
Labour	£ 90,000
Materials	£ 36,000
Plant Hire	£ 42,000
Permanent Way	£ 41,000
Signalling	£ 18,000
Total	£247,000

Grants and loans were received as follows:

Manpower Services Commission grant	£100,000
Wales Tourist Board – grant	£ 70,000
	£170,000

National Westminster Bank – loan free of interest for 1 year	£ 50,000

Gifts in kind, or services provided free or at reduced rates came from:

Imperial Chemical Industries	Sectional buildings
Messrs Thyssen (Great Britain) Ltd	Rock drills
Messrs Compair Construction & Mining Ltd	'Holbuster' equipment
Messrs Hymac	Loan of hydraulic excavator

A stockaded compound shortly appeared on the mountain slopes at a location known officially (but otherwise to nobody) as Glan-y-Llyn. Someone was unwise enough to suggest the name Fort Lewis and, not unnaturally, it stuck. How different it was to the volunteers' facilities; there were offices, mess rooms, canteen, stores, locker rooms, ladies' and gentlemen's toilets, office car, etc, all present and correct. Work began in October 1976, on receipt of official notification of the Wales Tourist Board grant.

Joe Bennion, MacAlpine's Site Engineer, when asked how the job would turn out, said modestly that he thought it would be a typical MacAlpine one; that is, finished to time, within budget, entirely to the customer's satisfaction. In a way, this was what happened and really it makes for very dull writing.

The original proposal was to break out the rock using some hydraulic hole-bursters (they use the enormous leverage possible with hydraulic pressure to crack open the rock at drilled holes) as rather low-power substitutes for gelignite; but with the hope of speeding things up, an experimental excavator-mounted giant power hammer (irreverently known as the 'donker') was lent to the project. 'When she was good she was very, very good, but when she was bad she was horrid', summed up the performance of Messrs Compair's 'Holbuster'. The proportion of 'horrid' time to 'good' time tended to increase as time went by, but no doubt the lessons learnt in Tan-y-Grisiau will by now have been applied by the manufacturers to what was basically an extremely powerful and useful piece of equipment. It was lent to the project on generous terms which really only met the firm's out-of-pocket expenses.

In compensation, the CEGB began to allow the use of explosives on the periphery of the prohibited area. Weekend work by volunteer Deviationists in places previously prohibited began to be allowed. This gradual erosion of the forbidden zones was achieved by a mixture of blackmail, cajolery, effrontery and application of the eleventh commandment ('Thou shalt not be found out'). Mr Golding of the Power Station said once to Mike Schumann 'It doesn't really matter what I say, you'll only do as you like.' It was a very pleasant turning of the tables compared with 20 years before.

Of course, the volunteers included by now many who were very experienced, while the staff engaged under the Job Creation Scheme were drawn from among the long-term unemployed in one of the United Kingdom's most depressed towns and were certainly not experienced or used to hard work. The Deviationists judged them very harshly but forget that, when a JCS man dodged the eagle eye of Tommy Hennigan, MacAlpine's archetypal Works Foreman, and spent an idle afternoon, he was getting the better of a system that had not brought much into his life; a Deviationist who did the same was only cheating himself. But a lot of the dedication disappeared, never properly to re-appear.

In early 1977, the MacAlpine contract was extended to take in the urgent work on the tunnel, in particular the portals over the entrances. An amazing 2ft gauge vehicle consisting basically of a revolving drum was hired from Thyssens of Cardiff, in order to carry ready-mixed concrete from the road access point near the power station down to the tunnel. A concrete pump was provided on-site to deliver the mix to the work from the rail-mounted drum. Overshadowing all this good news was that same Black Hole across the lake, ready to swallow anything or anyone who went near; this was the spectre of having to provide lining in the tunnel, the need for which was discussed in the last chapter. The problem really was this. Concrete spraying is a very specialised technique, mainly because spraying intrinsically means forcing a liquid through a small aperture; alas, concrete is not really a liquid; unfortunately it has stones in it. Consistency is very important, too; it has to be just right if the spray is to adhere correctly, or piles of waste just accumulate on the floor.

If you want to apply a specialised technique there are two choices – you either pay someone with experience to do the job for you or you do the job yourself, but expect to spend a certain period learning the technique. Alas, the Company had, as it were, hocked everything to get the Deviation built and extra funds were at a premium. They under-estimated the difficulties of learning the technique, while over-estimating the experience and abilities of their advisors and suppliers. One now suspects that the lost revenue caused by the delay in opening the tunnel in 1977 and also the late re-opening in 1978, might have paid for the extra costs of an experienced specialist contractor. But that is with the unfair advantage of hind-sight; at the time the decisions were taken they seemed the right ones.

The system chosen was the Norwegian SEM Wet Shotcreting Process, new to Britain but offered by Sykes Construction Services of Warrington. The spray gun atomised the concrete liquid by means of a jet of compressed air and there was provision to add agents at the nozzle to impart special last minute properties to the mix; in particular to cause the concrete to set instantaneously on contact with the rock and thereby adhere better. The cycle of spraying a load of ready-mix concrete satisfactorily depended, first, on there not being a single stone above about half-inch size in the concrete; second, on every item of plant functioning correctly – that is the plant at Minffordd Quarry; ready-mix lorries between the quarry and the rail transfer point; the drum wagon and locomotives (two were required to handle the weight) running down to the tunnel; the main compressor; the concrete pump; the pump for washing out and finally the lighting generators. The result was that, while the spraying of six loads of concrete a day was completely possible, this output was in fact achieved only once; the average was no more than two.

A noble contribution was a do-it-yourself drum wagon, made on the initiative of and largely by Andy Putnam, in order to save the cost of hiring one. He used ex-Polish State Railways bogies, an ex-Isle of Man Railway carriage underframe, a surplus concrete mixing drum from the Pwllheli Granite Co (which supplied the concrete) and a 'borrowed' diesel engine. He now says, however, that if the work had to be done again, it would be better to mix the concrete on site. Whenever one of those frequent malfunctions occurred and stopped spraying, the ready-mix load on hand had to be disposed of quickly before it set. At the same time a second load of ready-mix concrete would be on its way and this also would be wasted. Incidentally, the drum wagon has since earned more than its cost on hire to the contractors for the new pumped-storage hydro-electric scheme at Llanberis.

So the job of lining the tunnel took six months, from January to June 1978. It was a long and unpleasant task, made worse by endless frustrations and delays while experience was being gained, plus far more than a fair share of bad mechanical luck with the conventional items of equipment. To David Payne and Andy Putnam and their team, all praise for sticking to the ship and seeing the job through. Dave Payne, in fact, put his experience to good use afterwards in taking a post as shotcreting expert with Sykes Construction Services. It is a measure of the level which the team's expertise finally reached that a Shotcreting Open Day was held on 27 March; interested civil engineering people came from far afield and it was a very instructive and well organised occasion.

It is sad to note that the Project Engineer's job had now come full circle. Mike Schumann took on the job (with some reluctance) in order to have an adventure in construction, to lead bands of volunteers out to do battle with the rocks of Wales, leaving the paper-work and battles with bureaucracy behind. Now we find him as resident engineer to a big professional contract, occupied with what? – paper-work and battles with bureaucracy! Of course, this applies very much to the railway as a whole, the most vivid illustration being when, in the early 1970s, Allan Garraway had to give up driving his beloved locomotive *Linda*. He now needs to drive the General Manager's desk all day instead of just in the mornings.

A tower of strength to Chairman, General Manager, and Project Engineer during this period was the presence and counsel of Ben Ball. It was a time when so many decisions were not a question of choosing the best amongst good solutions, but the least bad amongst poor ones. In the circumstances a man who had (for example) been responsible for the communications planning for D-day in 1944 was one to have around. So it was a very sad day and a great loss to the Cause when, on 24 January, 1977, Sir Ben died after a short illness.

With this chapter containing so much that was a tale of woe, it is a pleasure to record that the last and best of the artifacts of the Deviation was a final triumph for the Schumann-Lewis-Deviationists combination. Paper-work and bureaucratic hassle were at a minimum, fun on site at a maximum. The Afon Cwmorthin bridge is also the only one which the public sees; the penstock bridges were buried, the tunnel is fundamentally just a dark hole, while one might happen to get a glimpse of Rhoslyn if one looks out of the observation car at just the right moment. But Afon Cwmorthin is close to the station at Tan-y-Grisiau, as well as to the CEGB's public reception centre and car park. One's eyes are irresistably drawn to the bridge by the magnificent waterfall that tumbles a few feet away. Do you think Mike or Bunny felt like Cecil Rhodes when he said that the Victoria Falls Bridge should be set so that 'the carriages are washed by the spray'? Like the Victoria Falls Bridge which was erected 20ft too low, Afon Cwmorthin Bridge was also put in the wrong place, leading to a little extra voluptousness in the curves on each side as well as some pleasurable intellectual exercise for the man who had to set them out.

At Easter 1976 the Deviationists did the main job of

concreting the abutments at each side, using ready-mixed concrete and a concrete pump. On 26 July, three great articulated lorries set off from Dow-Mac's Gloucester works, each with one 55ft long concrete beam marked 'ANOTHER CONCRETE BEAM FOR THE FESTINIOG RAILWAY EXTENSION' in huge letters. Francis Turner, the Deviation's stone-walling expert, painted the signs. On the following day a huge crane of nominal 100-ton capacity, but for this job rigged to give a long reach for a smaller load, stood way out to one side and picked the beams one by one off the lorries and placed them across the gap. The FR Guardian Angel was on hand too; a 50-ton crane had been ordered but the hirers substituted a 100-ton Unit at the 50-ton rate. On site, it was found that the capacity of the big crane was necessary!

The later stages of filling in the beams to make the deck, the parapets, railing cable ducts and other details, came along steadily, ready for tracklaying early in 1978. It was a fitting swan-song to the achievements of the Civil Engineering Group on the Deviation, and all done at the very modest cost of £6000.

12

Trains are running now

'We knocked the bastard off'
Sir Edmund Hilary   On climbing Everest, 1953

At precisely 12.06 on 24 June, 1978 the Hunslet 2-4-0 *Blanche* came off the Deviation and placed her lady-like pony wheels delicately on to the old Festiniog line at the north end of Tan-y-Grisiau station. The Deviationists had done it.

By John Routly's special instruction, all those who travelled on *Blanche*'s train had been active on Deviation construction. Other types of VIP had to wait for the No 2 train (*Merddin Emrys*) 30 minutes later. Traditional Deviation rain fell like stair rods but the speeches (normally 'things we chiefly bless when once we have got them over') were surprisingly good. Alan Pegler had crossed half the world to make his and Michael Schumann (brandishing the original 'first sod' spade) announced with relief he was standing down as project engineer. Allan Garraway spoke, while John Routly introduced Dewi Rees, Director of the Manpower Services Commission (and, accordingly, one of the Deviation's greatest benefactors), who then spoke to great effect in complimenting those who had done the work. He did his bit by driving home the golden spike with efficiency and panache. In fact it was copper plated and presented (knowingly or unknowingly, I wonder?) by a certain Canadian railroad via Festiniog Director Viscount Garnock.

Possibly the speakers spoke so well because they just had to offer something worthwhile to listeners standing in all that wet – although excellent wine presented to that huge gathering by Ffestiniog Director Bill Broadbent must also have had its effect. Anyway, the weather cheered up that evening for a mid-summer barbeque, including two sheep roasted whole, within the spiral at Dduallt. Public service to Tan-y-Grisiau began with the 15.00 train from Porthmadog and there was a further special, with a party of French enthusiasts, at 16.30.

For many of the Deviationists, 24 June was, as expected, a great anti-climax. No single afternoon's celebration could possibly live up to the years of hard work, achievement and fun. As the first 'first train' neared Tan-y-Grisiau Dick Davies turned to Chris Chitty and said, 'I didn't enjoy that, let's go and build a railway somewhere else!' and the whole carriage fell about laughing. When all was said and done, they had worked 16 months for every minute of train ride!

Chris Chitty writes:

> I gave up working for the Deviation this June (1979) because I feel I have done enough. I am not bitter about the situation at the end of the work, there had to be a winding-down, that was inevitable. I know that I probably got more out of the Deviation than I put into it and that is a hell of a lot. The Deviation has given me a vast social life, few enemies, a huge insight into human nature, plenty of civil engineering experience and the satisfaction of being involved in one of the most ambitious volunteer projects of all time – indeed, it was the forerunner of many schemes of a similar nature. I wouldn't have missed it for anything.

Even so, the party that evening at Dduallt was quite something; 195 Deviationists and their guests attended for the evening, plus Festiniog Society members who descended from their special train for long enough to drink a joint toast. It is on record that 63 litre bottles of wine were drunk, also 5 gallons of cider, 60 gallons of beer and 60 bottles of champagne. A night to remember.

In concentrating upon what the Civil Engineering Group did in producing a usable railway grade, the efforts of other departments in furnishing that grade have so far been ignored. The permanent way had to be set out, laid, ballasted, aligned and tamped, as well as being protected by two lines of sheep-proof fencing. To my friends Fred Howes, permanent way foreman, and Norman Gurley, new works ganger, all honour in producing 2½ miles of smooth and beautiful steel highway that would do credit to any railway in the world and which is quite a *non pareil* amongst tourist lines. They got the usual support from their permanent staff as well as generous assistance from that other lot of volunteers – the ones the Deviationists promised never to poach – hailing from the FR Society. The quantities of material involved in the last stages meant some real Trans-Atlantic style freight train operation, with such delights as a 100-ton 'hot-shot', triple-diesel-headed (*Moelwyn, Moel Hebog* and *Upnor Castle*) out of Minffordd to Head of Steel behind the power station, on 28 January, 1978.

Heavy second-hand 75lb flat bottom (with some new 60lb) rail was used, screwed and/or clipped to new Australian jarrah sleepers. An expensive proposal to introduce a nasty discontinuity by having concrete paved track in the tunnel was happily (to your author's mind – he was almost alone in opposing it) disposed of when time ran out during the events of early 1977. One case of an ill wind. . . .

The Deviation permanent way was a move away from the FR practice of staggering joints on curves. Staggered joints make a good 'line' (alignment) easier to maintain, but they are also more liable to introduce successively opposed variations in cross-level. It is the latter which can in the limit lift a wheel flange across a rail head, while a minor kink just does not look very nice and might at the worst spill a drop of coffee.

An interesting curiosity is the four-rail section behind the station where, in accordance with the Light Railway Order, outside guard rails protect all the volts and amps, not to speak of the tons of water pressure, from wild narrow-gauge trains running amok down the mountain side. Elm sleepers surplus from the reconstruction of the Glasgow Subway were used and in fact, by coincidence, the gauge across the guard rails approximates to the unusual 4ft gauge of that system.

A British Railways permanent way supervisor, Inspector Hill

of Ashchurch, once said to your author that track was like human life, needing all the attention at the beginning and at the end. Fred Howes faced the situation that, with the new line opening, far too much of his track was going to be at the infant stage at once. Now it just so happened (!) that Mike Elvy, a British Rail civil engineer in 1968 had got hold of an obsolete standard-gauge Matisa tamping machine, while Allan Garraway managed to get approval to buy it. It also just so happened that the rebuilding of this machine and its conversion to 1ft 11⅝in gauge came finally to fruition as the FR's *Stefcomatic* tamping machine, on 11 November 1977. Our old friend, that FR Guardian Angel, kindly motivated the right man – volunteer Steve Coulson, hence the name Stefcomatic – to take charge. Others involved were David Baskcomb, Warren Shepherd and Alan Stevens, all of Boston Lodge Works, as well, of course, as Paul Dukes, the works manager.

Boston Lodge Works is another institution to whom the success of the Deviation owes a great deal. On the whole, Blodge, as it is known, got little credit for what was done there in providing back-up to the civil engineering effort, only blame for rare failures. But they never wrought better than when they gave the FR a bright yellow automatic tamping machine just when it was wanted to consolidate the Deviation line. The trouble free running achieved in the first season owes a good deal to this triumph of mind over matter.

With Tan-y-Grisiau temporarily a terminus, signalling to enable trains to cross there is not yet needed but the Signal & Telegraph Department had to turn Dduallt into a crossing place involving a new signalbox and signals. The barriers and signalling for the two level crossings provided some headaches, not wholly resolved at the time of writing. Temporary hutted accommodation (ex Fort Lewis) provided a booking office, waiting room, shop and refreshment counter, as well as in two other buildings the 'usual facilities'. Management and office staff from Porthmadog temporarily had laid down their pens for mattocks and shovels in order to construct the platforms, in particular the concrete edging, during the winter. It reminded your author of a friend of his who went teaching in Ethiopia; because of over-crowding he asked the authorities for an extension to his school. Very well, they said, and promptly delivered him the bricks and mortar. All the un-appreciated (unless they get forgotten) but essential background things such as water supplies, plumbing, station seats, a water tank, platform lights, furniture, electrical wiring and other items which make up a working railway, also had to be obtained and set up.

And after all this, how did our Deviation do? Not so bad, in fact; the number of fare-paying passengers rose by 15 per cent in 1978 compared with pre-Deviation 1976, although 1978 was generally considered in North Wales to be a poor season. Revenue went up by a very satisfactory 73 per cent, reflecting a modest increase in rates corresponding to inflation but a sub-stantial effect from people making the longer journey. There were some overcrowding problems at the peak period, not surprising when the final passenger journey count was over 400,000.

The Association of Railway Preservation Societies makes an annual award to the one of its members who has made the most outstanding contribution to voluntary railway preservation. The actual trophy is a magnificent royal coat of arms in moulded relief, which long ago adorned the front of royal train locomotives on the London, Brighton & South Coast Railway. There was no question as to what the deed to be honoured in 1978 should be; the problem really was that the only eligible recipient, the Festiniog Railway Society, a member of the ARPS, really had by deliberate choice little to do with the Deviation. It was a slightly Gilbertian situation and, while ARPS proceedings often have a flavour of the opera *HMS Pinafore*, honour was satisfied by Mike Schumann going with Festiniog Society Chairman Gordon Caddy and Allan Garraway to York on 27 January 1979 to receive the award from Lord Downe.

The cost of the $2\frac{1}{2}$-mile Deviation had been very high, almost £610,000. The volunteer effort was valued at £180,000 over and above this, and various gifts another £25,000. Of the cost, the taxpayer should remember with gratitude the following bodies who spent his money in such a good cause:

Wales Tourist Board	£178,000
Development Board for Rural Wales	£42,500
Manpower Services Commission (Job Creation Scheme)	£142,000
Compensation from the CEGB (including interest)	£107,000

The remainder of the money was found out of the Company's revenue or borrowed, the latter being made less painful by the generosity of the National Westminster Bank Ltd, in granting a loan of £50,000 interest-free for a year. Even so, the Deviation was responsible for the FR's borrowings from the bank, being as high as £230,000 at the end of 1978. Aside and above this (and also aided to some extent by the taxpayer) must not be forgotten the extra rolling stock and motive power needed to provide the same frequency of service on the extended line as had been provided on the shorter one.

Furthermore, Tan-y-Grisiau is not Blaenau Ffestiniog and, while the route between them nominally exists, it is full of expensive problems. The new joint BR/FR station in the town is now a project to be funded independently of the Festiniog Railway and in due course will be the subject of a conventional civil engineering contract.

The original Deviationists envisaged disbanding themselves when the Deviation was finished, but Colin James, the new project engineer, has other ideas. Currently, of course, the Deviation is far from finished and Colin's people are occupied at the moment in a massive landscaping and tidy-up operation, as well as doing all those little things that just did not quite get done at the time. In designing such things as culverts, too, there is always an element of trial and error; storm water is cussed stuff and a number of alterations are having to be done. The mantle of Bunny Lewis has fallen on the broad shoulders of

Andy Putnam, who has also been having a little more full-time paid assistance on site. As a start, the Deviationists have become the Civil Engineering Group of the Festiniog Railway Society.

While the Festiniog Railway hardly needs Deviationists in the future, there is a great wide gap ready to be filled by a Civil Engineering Group. Before Tan-y-Grisiau can be linked to that million-pound railway complex in the centre of Blaenau Ffestiniog, eight bridges need to be reconstructed, quite apart from the one which the local authorities took down thinking they would never have to replace it (but have now had to). A nasty rock fall below the line needs remedial measures, once the experts agree whether to shore it up with a huge retaining wall or whether to set the line back further into the mountain side.

When the contemplated branch line to Dinas to serve the Llechwydd Quarry tourist complex, with its exciting things like underground inclines converted to funicular railways, comes to be built, there is a good deal to do there. Furthermore, one can see a need for one or two major bridge reconstructions in the future on the lower sections of the original main line.

Moving away slightly, Tan-y-Grisiau station, in one of the loveliest situations of any railway station in the world, is disfigured by buildings which are almost the nastiest lash-ups. As far as the Festiniog Railway is concerned, these temporary structures will have to be replaced, but problems of finance are likely to be as acute or even acuter than ever. With experience gained on stone culvert walls, could not the Civil Engineering Group put the final seal on their great work by constructing the station block there in traditional style?

However these matters turn out, nevertheless the iron resolve on the part both of those who serve and of those who control the company, to re-open and restore to perfection the whole of their historic line, is not likely to waver. Nor, having regard to what has been accomplished so far, are they likely to fail.

Above: Bunny Lewis supervises a pipe-rolling team building one of the culverts near the eventual site of Fort Lewis. *Ffestiniog Railway*
Below: With the power station only a few yards ahead a culvert is seen under construction. The Central Electricity Generating Board made it a condition that work should be done only under the supervision of a professional contracting firm, in this case Sir Alfred MacAlpine & Co. *FR Civil Engineering Group*

Above: The completed Afon Cwmorthin bridge with the spectacular waterfall just beyond the bridge. *FR Civil Engineering Group*
Below: Afon Cwmorthin bridge near Tan-y-Grisiau: a large 100-ton mobile crane makes easy work of the installation of the pre-stressed concrete beams which will carry the railway over the mountain stream flowing into the reservoir.

Appendix A
Decision of the Lands Tribunal

REF/144/1958

LANDS TRIBUNAL ACT 1949
IN THE MATTER OF A NOTICE OF REFERENCE
BETWEEN   FESTINIOG RAILWAY COMPANY   Claimants
and
CENTRAL ELECTRICITY GENERATING BOARD
Compensating Authority
Re: LIGHT RAILWAY BETWEEN BLAENAU
FFESTINIOG MERIONETH AND PORTMADOC
CAERNARVON

DECISION OF THE LANDS TRIBUNAL

This decision starts not with any of the issues raised during the hearing but with an explanation concerning spelling. The Railway Company came into being under an Act of 1832 and therein it is called The Festiniog Railway Company – Festiniog with but one 'f' – and so it has remained. The town and vale of Ffestiniog and in the name of the town Blaenau Ffestiniog the Welsh spelling is retained with a double 'f'.

This reference concerns the compensation to be paid by the Central Electricity Generating Board to the Festiniog Railway Company following the compulsory acquisition of a section of the railway by the

Board to enable them to construct a pumped storage reservoir in the valley south of Tan-y-Grisiau which involved flooding part of the track of the railway. Notice of entry was served on 3 February 1956 in respect of the section of the railway above Moelwyn Tunnel and on 4 June 1958 for the tunnel itself.

There was a hearing of this reference by the Lands Tribunal in 1960 where the sole issue was to determine the basis upon which compensation should be paid, the Company putting forward reinstatement (rule 5) which was contested by the Board. The Tribunal decided that rule 5 was not applicable. The case went forward to the Court of Appeal (1962 13P and C.R. 248) which on 2 February 1962 upheld the decision of the Lands Tribunal.

This further hearing is to determine the amount of that part of the compensation which arises out of disturbance, the value of the land having been agreed.

The history of the railway up to 1960 is set out in the decision of the Lands Tribunal dated 18 July 1960 and I need only carry the story forward from that date. In 1964 work began to extend services from Tan-y-Bwlch to Dduallt which is a little distance south of the Moelwyn Tunnel and where there is no road access. This stretch of the railway was opened in 1968 and Dduallt is still the northern terminus. From 1958 to 1968 traffic increased at the rate of about 10 per cent a year; in 1968 the increase was 33 per cent, and for 1969 and 1970 the average annual increase was about 10 per cent.

The loss of the section of the railway embraced by the compulsory purchase order did not damp the resolve of the claimant Company eventually to re-open the railway right up to Blaenau Ffestiniog, and in this the Company were enthusiastically supported by the Festiniog Railway Society which had been formed in 1951 with the object of re-opening the railway. The membership of the Society has grown steadily and the Society has contributed gifts of money to the railway and its members, now some 5,400, have contributed both skilled and unskilled labour for the restoration of the railway. During the hearing I was told that a Charitable Trust hold the shares in the Company and the debentures in trust to hold for the same purpose as the objects of the Society.

In 1957–58 a scheme was drawn up on behalf of the Company for the diversion of the railway to the west of the reservoir (the 'Goode route') but this was unacceptable to the Board. The Company then proposed the diversion of the railway to the east of the reservoir (the 'Livesey and Henderson route'), and this was the diversion considered in the Lands Tribunal proceedings in 1960. After the decision of the

Court of Appeal in 1962, the Company drew up a revised version of the eastern route [the 'Fox route']. Planning permission was granted for this route in June 1965. The construction of the diversion then began with a spiral at Dduallt Station. The Company applied to the Ministry of Transport for a Light Railway Order. Objections were received from two land owners and (for protective purposes) from the Central Electricity Generating Board. An inquiry into objections was held on 26–27 January 1967; the Board withdrew their objection at the inquiry on agreed terms. The Ministry approved the Light Railway Order on 9 February, 1968 and the order came into operation on 21 February, 1968. There followed proceedings for the purchase by the Company of land required for the diversion route and in the case of one ownership determination was made by the Lands Tribunal (L.C.A./49/1968) under Section 85 of the Lands Clauses Consolidation Act 1845 (which is the section which allows entry on and use of, land before purchase on making deposit by way of security and giving bond).

Before applying for the further Light Railway Order required to carry the railway over the dam at the northern end of the reservoir, the Company wrote on 7 October, 1968 to the Board requesting that the question of a diversion to the west of the reservoir be reconsidered. Following correspondence and meetings, agreement was reached and by letter dated 20 September, 1971 the Board confirmed its acceptance of the proposed west side route subject to conditions relating to detail. These conditions, in fact, were agreed before the end of the hearing but as I do not think that they affect any of the issues in this case I am not referring to them again.

For the purpose of these proceedings it is agreed that it shall be assumed that planning permission will be granted for the new west route and it is upon the assumption that the railway will in due course reach Blaenau Ffestiniog by this west route that the calculations relating to the claim in respect of disturbance have been made by both parties.

Evidence for the claimants was given by Mr A. G. W. Garraway, MA, Eng, the general manager of the railway company, who dealt with the assumptions made by the Company in the formulation of the claim for loss of profit, the running of the railway, the repairs and maintenance both current and deferred, the improvements made to the line, buildings and rolling stock, in short, all matters pertaining to the operation of the railway including work on the proposed new west route. Mr A. Ll. Lambert, the Managing Director of the Festiniog Railway Society, informed me concerning the Society, Mr T. Mervyn

Jones, MA, LLB, CBE, the Chairman of the Welsh Tourist Board, drew my attention to the importance to the tourist industry of Wales of the "great little trains" of the principality, particularly the Festiniog Railway and the additional attraction that this railway would have once the line was open for the full length from Portmadoc to Blaenau Ffestiniog. Mr L. J. W. Smith, MTPI, partner in Chas. R. Lowe & Co and the director of the Festiniog Railway Company, in charge of property and works, gave evidence concerning the alternative routes of diversion following the compulsory acquisition and the work entailed therein and the necessity for the further Light Railway Order which includes the recently agreed west route. Mr W. G. B. Walker, FCA, partner in Peat Marwick Mitchell & Co chartered accountants, dealt with the calculations of loss of profit including the discounting factor applicable to future profits, the division of maintenance between current and deferred maintenance, and to which account the deferred maintenance should be debited. Lastly, Mr E. J. Routley, MA, Deputy Chairman of the Company and Chairman of the Board of Directors, whose evidence was primarily concerned with explaining how the Directors divided expenditure on maintenance between current and deferred maintenance.

Evidence for the Board was given by Mr S. W. Hill, Chartered Municipal Treasurer, a partner in Arthur Collins & Co., who dealt with the actual profits and the hypothetical profits had the line been opened and remained open to Blaenau Ffestiniog without the truncation of the Board and from these figures calculated the loss of profits suffered by the Company, and he also dealt with the risk rates which should be applied in formulating the claim.

Colonel D. McMullen, CBE, FICE, consultant in Freeman Fox & Partners, spoke of the inspection of the railway which he had made following applications from the Company for authority to open sections of the line to passenger traffic. He gave his view concerning the date by which the whole line, that is from Portmadoc to Blaenau Ffestiniog might have opened but for the intervention of the Board, the number of journeys which could be made bearing in mind the rolling stock available and the time required to turn trains round.

I am not going to follow my normal practice of setting out in detail the evidence given by each witness partly because there was overlapping, partly because of the mass of detail, but primarily because I think it best to consider each main item of the claim and at that stage indicate whether the parties and their witnesses agree or disagree.

First, however, I should say something about the Company and its accounts. From the evidence I have been satisfied that the Company are not concerned with the payment of dividends, any profit arising being ploughed back. In September 1954, when the work of restoration began, the track and rolling stock were in a derelict state and work commenced with a small permanent staff and a large body of volunteers. Throughout the years up to today, and I think in the future, the maintenance work necessary for current wear and tear, for restoration work and for new works has and will be done by a small permanent staff, now about 40, assisted by a great number of volunteers.

On the accountancy side up to 1963 the cost of all maintenance was charged against the receipts in the revenue account. For the year 1963 and onwards, however, a change was made and there is now an 'operating account' showing the receipts for the year on the credit side and on the debit side the cost of current maintenance, locomotive running expenses, traffic expenses, general charges, and miscellaneous expenditure. The balance of the operating account is taken to a 'revenue appropriation account' and the expenditure on deferred maintenance is charged to this appropriation account. This way of dealing with maintenance costs which was not challenged by the Board necessitates, however, a splitting of the total into its two parts. This is not done by a meticulous enquiry into figures but is decided by the Board in the light of information given by senior officials, all the members of the Board having an extensive knowledge of the railway and its running. The apportionment is reviewed each year, in practice, however, whereas in 1963 and 1964, one-third of the total was allocated to current maintenance and two-thirds to deferred maintenance from 1965 onwards the total cost has been equally divided. In 1970, however, I was told there was exceptional expenditure on deferred maintenance and the sum of £10,000 was allocated to deferred and only then was the balance split evenly.

I now set out the first page of the claimants' document C.12 which consists of the 'Summary of Claim'.

A. 1962–1976 Loss of Profit

I. 1962–1970	£116,929
II. 1971–1976	113,922
	230,851
Deduct Taxation at 40 per cent	92,340
Loss of Profit	£138,511

B. 1977 – Capitalised value of additional cost due to
   alternative route   8,322
C. Preliminary expenses in establishing alternative
   route   5,228

                                                       £152,061

The first item A.I shows a loss of profit for the years 1962 to 1970 as £116,929. This is arrived at by deducting the profit shown in the accounts, totalling £137,438 from estimated profits on the assumption that there had been no disturbance, £254,367.

Both parties ignore certain relatively small sums of miscellaneous receipts and expenditure in their calculations and I shall not refer to them.

The claimants have made an adjustment in the accounts for 1962 and for the purpose of the above calculation they have divided the maintenance expenditure one-third to current and two-thirds to deferred. Mr Hill in his evidence for the Board did not question the profit figures for 1962–70 save in one very important respect. He agrees the claimant's figures so far as they go but in his view it is wrong to arrive at a profit figure without bringing into account the expenditure on deferred maintenance. This, of course, makes a striking difference as will be seen from the comparable figures of loss of profit which are set out a little later in this decision. Mr Hill's figures are only from 1965 onwards as he was advised that the Company would not have been enabled to operate up to Blaenau Ffestiniog until that year.

The next matter which was considered was the estimated profits which could have arisen had there been no interruption of re-opening of the entire line. The Company set out six assumptions upon which their calculations were based:

1. Passenger journeys would have been 30 per cent greater.

The claimants supported the 30 per cent by reference to the increase in the year when the line was extended to Dduallt in 1968. The Board conceded a 30 per cent increase but thought that the correct interpretation of earlier increases in traffic following extensions of the railway was that the increase would have been gradual and Mr Hill gave an increase of 20 per cent for 2 years, 25 per cent for the third year and 30 per cent for the 4th year and onwards.

2. The average number of miles travelled by each passenger would have been 11. This was agreed.

3. The average passenger receipts per passenger mile would have been at their actual level.

There is no dispute here, both parties adopting the same fare per passenger mile.

4. Profits on goods sold would have increased by the increased percentage of journeys.

This is agreed, but Mr Hill of course applies his lesser percentages for the earlier years.

5. Current maintenance, locomotive running and traffic expenses would have increased in proportion to passenger miles.

This is adopted by both parties except for 'deferred maintenance' where Mr Hill takes a track ratio, 13/10. Portmadoc to Blaenau is roughly 13 miles of track and to Dduallt 10 miles. The Company do not include deferred maintenance in their revenue expenditure so have no corresponding item.

6. General charges would have been 25 per cent greater than actual. This is agreed.

In his calculations concerning the hypothetical profits with the line extended to Blaenau Ffestiniog Mr Hill not only makes deductions for deferred maintenance but also increases the special expenditure in 1970 from £10,000 (as in the accounts) to £12,000 and for the years 1968 to 1970 makes a deduction for additional rates of £4,000 on the ground that the extension of the line would have been bound to have been followed by a review of the rating assessment resulting in an increase in the rateable value. If the claimants' figures for receipts and expenditure were to be accepted then he said the deduction for additional rates should be £6,343.

The corresponding figures for the claimants and the Board thus far are here set out for ease of comparison.

LOSS OF PROFITS BEFORE TAX

Claimant				Board			
		hypo-thetical extended				hypo-thetical extended	
	actual	line	loss		actual	line	loss
	£	£	£		£	£	£
1962	5,895	12,552	6,657				
1963	7,860	15,460	7,600				
1964	9,062	18,758	9,696				

1965	8,801	17,264	8,463	1,701	6,459	4,758
1966	8,031	16,321	8,290	(L)538	3,532	4,070
1967	15,600	29,853	14,253	5,818	15,627	9,809
1968	25,522	45,226	19,704	13,677	25,816	12,149
1969	28,182	50,666	22,484	11,380	24,825	13,445
1970	28,485	48,267	19,782	(L)3,400	3,817	7,217
	£137,438	£254,367	£116,929	£28,628	£80,076	£51,448

I now come to A.II, the loss of profit for the years 1971–76. Happily it is agreed that the alternative route from Dduallt to Blaenau Ffestiniog should be ready for use by 1977 and so 1976 is the last year to be used for the measure of loss of profit. It is also agreed that for these future years revenue and expenses may be regarded as remaining constant at the average levels of the 3 years 1968–70.

Mr Walker for the claimants naturally starts from his average loss of profit which is £20,657 and he takes this figure for 1971. To get to a present value for the subsequent years he uses a discounting factor of $3\frac{1}{2}$ per cent net of tax and the resulting total is £113,922. Mr Hill, using his figures for the years 1968–70, makes the average figure of loss of profits £11,000 per annum.

Both parties deduct taxation at 40 per cent.

Mr Hill, however, makes a further calculation and both for the 1965–70 period and for 1971–76 relates his figures for loss of profit back to 1956 and uses a $12\frac{1}{2}$ per cent risk rate which net of tax he gives as $7\frac{1}{2}$ per cent and this reduces the loss of profits for the years 1965–70 to £13,906 and for the years 1971–76 to £11,286 and he arrives at a total of £24,382.

Comparative figures for Part A of the claim are therefore for the Company £138,511 and for the Board £24,382.

I now come to item B in the claim, 1977 – capitalised value of additional cost due to alternative route £8,322.

The assumptions made by the Company concerning this part of the claim are:

1. The railway would operate to Blaenau Ffestiniog from 1977 using an alternative route of increased length.
2. The increased track mileage gives rise to increased costs (excluding general expenses) in perpetuity proportionate to passenger mileage.

They say that whereas the old route was 12·8 miles long the new route will be 13·5 miles, an increase of 5·5 per cent, which if applied to their estimate of costs for 1970, assuming the old route but excluding general expenses (£70,952) gives £3,902. This figure they reduce to the proportion which the average length of journey taken in 1970 bears to the maximum possible journey at 1970 (87·4 per cent) giving £3,410. This is capitalised by applying 3 years purchase (£10,230) and discounted to give a present value using a factor of $3\frac{1}{2}$ per cent and so produces their final figure of £8,332.

The whole of this item is refuted by the Board on legal grounds with which I will deal later, and also by the evidence of Mr Hill who said that in his view the track of the alternative route would be new and so would require less maintenance; he thought the new route would be more attractive than the old and this would influence the receipts and moreover if the Company continued to charge according to the length of journey the additional mileage would produce higher receipts and indeed extra revenue could exceed any increase in expenditure.

Concerning item C of the claim, preliminary expenses in establishing the alternative route, £5,228, the amount was not at issue as a figure but the Board submitted that on legal grounds the item was inadmissable.

Mr E. S. Fay, QC, on behalf of the Board, said that whilst he was not proposing to argue the point before the Tribunal, he reserved the right to submit to a Higher Court that it was inadmissable to refer to events happening subsequent to the entry on the land by the Board.

With regard to both B and C in the claim, Mr Fay submitted that neither of these items was allowable and referred to *Harvey* v *Crawley Development Corporation (1957 1 Q.B. 485)*. The claimants he said *choose* to make an alternative route to Blaenau Ffestiniog. This was a matter of choice and should not be regarded as a direct consequence flowing from the truncation of the railway, and furthermore here the Court of Appeal in this very case (13 P. & C.R. 248) had decided that reinstatement was not commercially feasible. Whilst he did not suggest that the making of the alternative route was unreasonable anything arising therefrom was outside the purview of these proceedings.

Turning to A, the loss of profits, he submitted that on the authority of *West Midlands Baptist Association v Birmingham Corporation (1970 A.C. 874)*, compensation was payable in this case at the date of dispossession, 1956, disturbance was part of the compensation *(Horn v Sunderland Corporation (1941 2 K.B. 46))* and under section 11 (1) of the Compulsory Purchase Act 1965 interest on the compensation had to be paid from the date of taking possession.

Mr David Widdicombe, QC, submitted on behalf of the claimants that item C of the claim (preliminary expenses in establishing alternative route) was not too remote and was the natural, direct and reasonable consequence of the dispossession and on the authority of *Harvey v Crawley* should be allowed.

Concerning B (1977 – capitalised value of additional cost due to alternative route) he said this was a capitalisation of permanent additional cost arising out of the truncation of the line and compensation fell to be paid therefore and he referred me to *B. & T. Essex Limited v Shoreditch Corporation* (9 P. & C.R. 471).

In his submission *Bwllfa & Merthyr Dare Steam Collieries Limited v Pontypridd Water Works Co* (1903 A.C. 426) and *London County Council v Tobin* (1959 1 W.L.R. 354) were authorities for taking into account factors known at the date of the hearing.

Mr Widdicombe argued that it was right to find the capital amount applicable to loss of profits on evidence available up to the date of the hearing, but it was wrong to discount that amount by applying thereto multipliers in order to discount to 1956 and he referred me to the Judgment of Lord Reid in the *West Midlands* case (1970 A.C. 874) where particularly at the bottom of page 896 he said,

'The actual costs of losses following on actual dispossession have been taken, and that appears to be the accepted practice today with regard to claims under Rule 6'.

I have inspected the line, workshops, and stations of the Festiniog Railway and also the Ffestiniog Power Station and the upper and lower reservoirs of the Board.

I will deal with the items of claim in the reverse order, taking first 'C' which was referred to during the hearing as 'Crawley costs'.

When the railway was severed by the Board acquiring a section north of Dduallt the Company could do one of two things, either they could run the line as near to the entrance of the Moelwyn Tunnel as feasible and go no further, or they could devise an alternative route which would enable them to reach Blaenau Ffestiniog. They decided to do the latter and the Board agreed that this was a reasonable course of action. In my view the preliminary expenses in establishing the alternative route are not too remote and are the natural, direct and reasonable consequence of dispossession. It was argued that the alternative route could not be taken into account in this claim for disturbance by reason of the decision of the Court of Appeal upholding the Lands Tribunal in its ruling that the cost of reinstatement did not afford a reasonable basis for compensation. This argument seems to me to go contrary to all the judgments in the *Crawley* case. The decision to go forward with an alternative line to Blaenau Ffestiniog, in my view, differs fundamentally from the 'choices' referred to by Denning LJ in the *Crawley* case where on page 493 he was illustrating the type of choice of action which would not qualify for inclusion in a disturbance claim; a house owned as an investment, compensation money invested in stock and shares and so forth.

The figure is not at issue and £5,228 will therefore be allowed under heading C.

Heading B sets out the sum of £8,322 being the capitalised value of additional cost due to the alternative route. It is true that the alternative route will be a little longer than the old route but the evidence has satisfied me that the receipts will more than cover any additional costs. The Company have failed to persuade me that their profits will be reduced due to having to use the alternative route. Accordingly this item is not allowed.

I now come to A, loss of profits 1962–76 and I think that first I should state that I consider that I am entitled on the authority of the *Bwllfa* case to have regard both to the accounts and to works done after 1956 up to the date of the hearing.

Though the point was reserved by Mr Fay for the Board both parties presented evidence involving matters right up to the hearing – the new alternative west route only became the agreed basis for compensation just before the hearing.

I start with A.I in the claim being that part which relates to the years 1962–70 and here there is an issue concerning the date by which the Company would have been able to open the old line right up to Blaenau but for the intervention by the Board: 1960, 1962 or 1964–65. Whilst I fully appreciate the knowledge and experience from which Colonel McMullen speaks I think he has underestimated the enthusiasm of those who work for the Company, whether they be directors, paid staff or voluntary workers and that his date of 1964 is too pessimistic, I prefer the evidence of Mr Garraway and find that had there been no acquisition 1962 is a reasonable date to take for the opening of the whole of the old line from Portmadoc to Blaenau Ffestiniog.

Would the passenger journeys have increased immediately by 30 per cent? Mr Mervyn Jones told me of the attraction to the tourist of the 'great little trains of Wales' and gave it as his opinion that once the Festiniog Railway ran its full length and so obtained convenient facilities at each end the tourist attraction would be greatly enhanced. This I would not question but I am concerned with the time it would take to achieve the increase in passenger journeys and I find that the past experience of the Company supports a stepped increase rather than an immediate increase to the full and I take 20 per cent for the first year, 25 per cent for the second year and 30 per cent for the third year and subsequently.

It is agreed that the average miles travelled by each passenger would have been 11 and that the average passenger receipts would have been at their actual level. I increase the profits on goods sold by the same percentage as I have found for the passenger journeys. It is agreed that current maintenance, locomotive running and traffic expenses would have increased in proportion to passenger miles and that general charges would have been 25 per cent greater than actual.

To what extent, if any, should deferred maintenance be deducted before arriving at profit?

As I understand the evidence the cost of deferred maintenance was, and is, met partly by gifts from the Society but mainly out of the actual profits arising from the running of the railway. In a good year more money was available and in a poor year less. The Board agreed that it was not a wrong method of accounting to show deferred maintenance as a charge against the revenue appropriation account rather than in the operating account. I think that this is correct and that it is not right to reduce the operating profit by increasing the current maintenance by the amount spent on deferred maintenance.

The term 'deferred maintenance' as it is used in this case includes the cost of restoring the assets which in 1954 were all in a very poor state and also the cost of alterations and improvements which, from the evidence given by Mr Garraway, were by no means insignificant. The alterations and improvements I regard as capital expenditure. Here restoration is financed primarily out of actual profits, but as suggested during the hearing, it could have been financed by the raising of a fund for that purpose specifically and had that been done it would not have affected the operating profits.

What has to be found is the loss suffered by the Company due to the intervention by the Board. The Company were prevented from making the profits which would have arisen from the operation of the full length of the line in 1962 and only in 1977 can they expect to reach Blaenau. They should be compensated for this loss. Since deferred maintenance is financed mainly out of operating profits the loss of these profits has restricted the amount of deferred maintenance which could be undertaken, the necessity for doing this maintenance remains but it will be longer before it can be completed.

There was criticism regarding the way in which the Company split their total maintenance cost as between current and deferred. I have already described how the apportionment was made and all I need say here is that I have been satisfied that the apportionment, made as it is by those who have an intimate knowledge of the railway is fair and reasonable.

In calculating the profits which would have arisen if the Board had not taken part of the original line Mr Hill makes a deduction for the years 1968–70 of £4,000 per annum for extra rates. The present rating assessment which has effect from 1963 was agreed with the Valuation Officer in June 1966 and no increase was made when the use of the railway was extended in 1968 to Dduallt. I think that had the old line been opened right up to Blaenau this would have attracted the attention of the Local Authority and also the Valuation Officer. Mr Hill deducts a figure of £4,000 for each of the three years but says that if the claimants figures for loss of profit are adopted the additional rates would amount to £6,343. Whilst agreeing that it would be reasonable to expect an increase in the rate payment the amount thereof is I think somewhat speculative, and though I have had the advantage of having Mr Hill's calculations put before me these however were challenged, at least as far as the tenants' share was concerned. I have decided to deduct £5,000 for each of the three years.

As I shall not be concerning myself with a deduction for deferred maintenance I shall not be concerned with the £10,000 of special expenditure in 1970 still less with the increase to £12,000 made by Mr Hill in which my view is unfounded.

A deduction of 40 per cent for tax is agreed.

I now come to A.II, in the claim which relates to loss of profits for the years 1971–1976. It is agreed that for these years it shall be assumed that the revenue and expenditure will remain constant at the average levels of the three years, 1968–70. At issue is the discounting factor to be used to bring the future years to present value; $3\frac{1}{2}$ per cent net of tax per Mr Walker or $7\frac{1}{2}$ per cent net of tax per Mr Hill.

This raises the wider question should this risk rate be applied only to profits lost in the years 1971–76 as done by the claimants or should it be applied in discounting the loss of profits from 1962 to 1976 back to 1956 as done by the Board?

In the *West Midlands Baptist* case (1970 A.C. 871) on page 899 Lord Reid said, 'Sometimes possession is taken before compensation is assessed. Then it would seem logical to fix the market value of the land as at that date and to take actual consequential losses as they occurred then or thereafter, provided the dispossessed owner had acted reasonably'. This at first sight might be taken as supporting the view that for the years 1962–70 the calculated loss of profit for each year should be taken and only the years 1971-76 discounted, but on p. 897 Lord Reid says, '. . . for it has been said again and again from an early date that there is only one subject for compensation – the value of the land to the owner. And it could not be right to value one element of the value to the owner, the market value of the land as at one date, and to value other elements, consequential losses, as at a different date. . . .'

In my view the loss of profits must be discounted to the time when the Board took possession of the land, which throughout the hearing has been taken, and I think rightly, as 1956 the date of the first entry for it is at this date that the compensation has to be assessed, and it is from this date that the Board will have to pay interest under Sec. 11 (1) of the Compulsory Purchase Act.

I will now deal with the issue between the parties concerning the discounting rate.

Mr Walker says that all known risks have been taken into account when arriving at the figures of annual loss of profit and accordingly any discounting which he only applies to the years 1971–76, should be at a rate appropriate to a risk-free income, $3\frac{1}{2}$ per cent net of tax. Mr Hill maintains that however careful one may have been, there are and must be imponderables when considering not only future possible profits but also loss of profit relating to past years for although one element, actual profit, is known, the profit arising if the old line had been opened to Blaenau is and must be a matter of estimation hence he uses $7\frac{1}{2}$ per cent net of tax.

Although great care has been taken in the estimation of the year by year loss of profit the resultant figures cannot be taken as certain, an element of risk does remain but I would not put it as high as $7\frac{1}{2}$ per cent net of tax. The Company have a good record of actual operating profits and I see no reason why the trend shown by past results should not go forward into the future. I shall take a rate of 5 per cent net of tax.

It was suggested by the Board that account ought to be had to a saving which had accrued to the Company because they did not now have to spend money bringing into repair the section of the line acquired by the Board. I do not agree for although the Company have been saved this cost they have to incur far greater expense in order that the line shall reach Blaenau. Had the claim been based upon permanent termination of the line at or about Dduallt there might have been a case for taking into account this saving but on both sides the case has proceeded on the assumption that the alternative route would be used; the Company do so specifically and the Board by inference as they cease the period for loss of profit at 1976 it being agreed that Blaenau would be reached and the line opened in 1977.

Following what I have laid down and adopting the form in which the Claimants presented this claim I find the figures to be:

A. 1962–1976. Loss of profits less tax at 40 per cent   £59,693

B. 1977 – Capitalised value of additional cost due to alternative route   nil

C. Preliminary expenses in establishing alternative route   £5,228

Compensation for disturbance   £64,921

say . . .   £65,000

That part of the compensation attributable to disturbance will accordingly be £65,000.

The Compensating Authority will pay to the Claimants their costs of this reference, such costs unless agreed to be taxed by the Registrar of the Lands Tribunal on the High Court Scale.

DATED this 19th day of November 1971

(Signed) H. P. HOBBS

APPEARANCES: Mr David Widdicombe, QC, and Mr Guy Seward of Counsel.

Instructed by Messrs Kenneth Brown Baker Baker Solicitors of London for Claimants.

Mr E. S. Fay, QC, and Mr Reginald Bell of Counsel Instructed by Solicitor to Central Electricity Generating Board for Authority.

HEARD: London 4th, 5th, 6th, 7th, 8th, and 11th October, 1971.

Appendix B
Extracts from Light Railway Orders of 1968 and 1975

1968   No 178

TRANSPORT

The Festiniog Railway (Light Railway) (Amendment)
Order 1968

Made   9 February 1968
Coming into Operation   21 February 1968

The Minister of Transport (hereinafter referred to as 'the Minister')
on the application of the Festiniog Railway Company (hereinafter
referred to as 'the Company') and in exercise of the powers conferred
upon her by sections 7, 9, 10 and 24 of the Light Railways Act 1896
as amended by the Light Railways Act 1912 (b) and Part V of the
Railways Act 1921 and of all other powers enabling her in that behalf
hereby makes the following Order:-

Citation and commencement

1. (1) This Order may be cited as the Festiniog Railway (Light
Railway) (Amendment) Order 1968 and shall come into operation on
the 21 February, 1968.

   (2) This Order and the Festiniog Railway (Light Railway) Order
1923 may be cited together as the Festiniog Light Railway Orders
1923 and 1968.

Power to make railway

4. (1) Subject to the provisions of this Order the Company may
make and maintain the railway hereinafter described in the lines and
according to the levels and within the limits of deviation shown on the
plans and sections and with all proper rails, plates, sidings, junctions,

Right: A train approaches the site of Llyn Ystradau temporary terminus. The breached dam of the reservoir which provided water power for working the original 1836 incline is seen in the background. In front of it is the CEGB's measuring weir. *Dan Wilson*

Below: *Earl of Merioneth*, the newest of the Ffestiniog Railway Fairlie locomotives, running on manicured permanent way, approaches the Stylwan dam road level crossing on the completed section of the deviation in 1979. *Brian Hollingsworth*

Right: Final act in the actual construction of the deviation was the ceremonial driving of the golden spike at Tan-y-Grisiau station on 24 June 1978. *FR Civil Engineering Group*

Below: *Earl of Merioneth* crosses Afon Cwmorthin bridge shortly after leaving Tan-y-Grisiau station. Although the deviation is now complete, at the time of going to press there is still much to be done before the line can be reopened throughout from Tan-y-Grisiau to the new planned station at Blaenau Ffestiniog. *Brian Hollingsworth*

bridges, culverts, drains, approaches, roads, yards, buildings and other works and conveniences connected therewith.

(2) The said railway is situate wholly in the urban district of Ffestiniog in the county of Merioneth and is –

a railway (No. 3) 1 mile 7 furlongs and 9 chains or thereabouts in length commencing by a junction with the principal railway at a point immediately to the north of Dduallt Station passing thence round the hill to the east of the said station crossing the principal railway by a bridge at a point 10 chains or thereabouts measured in a southerly direction from the point of commencement thence proceeding in a westerly, northwesterly and northerly direction to Coed Dduallt, thence in a northeasterly direction towards the principal railway thence in a northerly direction along the west side of the principal railway thence in a northeasterly and easterly direction crossing the Moelwyn Tunnel forming part of the principal railway thence in a southeasterly and easterly direction to Clogwyn thence in a general northwesterly and northerly direction to and terminating near Brookes Quarry on the eastern side of Llyn Ystradau.

Abandonment of part of principal railway

5. The Company shall not later than the completion and opening for public traffic of railway (No. 3) abandon and discontinue such part of the principal railway as is situate between a point approximately twenty-eight chains north of the commencement of railway (No. 3) and a point corresponding to the southern end of the part of the principal railway which has been acquired by the Central Electricity Generating Board and the powers of the Company in relation thereto shall cease.

Power to take lands

6. Subject to the provisions of this Order the Company may enter upon, take and use such of the lands shown on the plans described in the deposited book of reference as may be required for the purposes of railway (No. 3).

As to user of railway

7. No part of Railway (No. 3) shall be used for the public conveyance of passengers without the permission in writing of the Minister first being had and obtained which permission shall not be withheld if the Minister is satisfied that such use will not be attended with danger to the public, and the Company shall comply with the conditions (if any) which the Minister may from time to time prescribe for the safety of the public using railway (No. 3).

For protection of Central Electricity Generating Board

8. For the protection of the Board the following provisions shall, unless otherwise agreed in writing between the Company and the Board apply and have effect:-

(1) In this section unless the subject or context otherwise requires:-
'the Board' means the Central Electricity Generating Board.

(2) Notwithstanding anything in section 21 (Power to deviate) of the order of 1923 as applied to railway (No. 3) by section 3 (Application of parts of Order of 1923) of this Order or shown on the deposited plans the Company shall not in making the material section of the railway deviate laterally beyond the limits of deviation shown on the signed plan.

(3) (a) The Company shall make and maintain the following works for the accommodation of the Board as the owners of the protected land:

(i) a bridge over the material section of the railway between the points marked 'A' and 'B' on the signed plan or in such other position as may be determined suitable for use for any purpose and of such dimensions, method of construction and materials as may be determined;

(ii) a crossing over the material section of the railway at such point as may be determined suitable for use for agricultural purposes and of such dimensions, method of construction and materials as may be determined;

(iii) a fence to separate so much of the protected land as is not acquired by the Company for the purpose of making and maintaining the material section of the railway from the remainder of that land such fence to be erected on either side of and across the termination of the said section in such position and of such a type as may be determined.

(4) No station or other facilities for passengers to board or alight from trains shall be constructed or provided on the protected land.

(5) No explosives shall be used in connection with the making or maintaining of the material section of the railway except at such places and in accordance with such terms and conditions (including conditions relating to the making of excavations in which the explosives are to be placed) as may be approved in writing by the Board.

(6) No spoil or other materials obtained from the making and maintaining of railway (No. 3) shall be deposited on the

protected land except in such positions and subject to such terms and conditions as may be agreed in writing between the Company and the Board or, in default of agreement, as may be approved by the National Parks Commission.

(7) (a) The Board shall be entitled to place electric lines (as defined in the Electric Lighting Act 1882 on, over or under any part of the protected land in such position and subject to such terms and conditions as may be determined.

(8) The Board shall not be liable for any damage to the material section of the railway due either directly or indirectly to erosion of the bank of the reservoir (Work No. 3) authorised by the North Wales Hydro-Electric Power Act 1955.

(9) (a) The Company shall before commencing to construct any part of the material section of the railway submit to the Board for their reasonable approval plans thereof and of any temporary works to be constructed on the protected land, and in giving their approval the Board shall be entitled to take into account the effect on the amenities of the area of the construction of the material section of the railway;

(b) If the Board do not within fifty-six days after the submission to them of any such plans signify to the Company in writing their approval or disapproval thereof they shall be deemed to have approved thereof;

(c) No part of the material section of the railway shall be constructed otherwise than in accordance with such plans as may have been approved (or deemed to have been approved) by the Board or if such approval be withheld as may be settled by arbitration and any such work shall be executed to the reasonable satisfaction of the Board.

(10) The Company shall at all times keep the Board indemnified against all damages, losses, costs and expenses which they may sustain or be liable for or reasonably and properly incur by reason or in consequence of any injury, damage or interference which may be caused or may result

(a) to any property of the Board in the exercise of any powers conferred by this Order;

(b) to any person travelling on or employed in connection with the material section of the railway due either directly or indirectly to erosion of the bank referred to in paragraph (8):

Provided that the Board shall give to the Company notice of

any claim or demand made against them which in the opinion of the Board is a claim or demand for which the Company may be liable under this paragraph and no settlement or compromise of any such claim or demand shall be made without the consent in writing of the Company.

(11) The fact that any work or thing has been executed or done in accordance with a plan approved or deemed to be approved by the Board or to their satisfaction or in accordance with any directions or award of an arbitrator shall not relieve the Company from any liability under the provisions of this section.

(12) Except as may be otherwise expressly provided by this section any difference arising under this section between the Company and the Board (other than a difference as to the meaning or construction thereof) shall be referred to and determined by an arbitrator to be appointed by agreement between the Company and the Board or, failing agreement on the application of either party after notice in writing to the other by the President of the Institution of Civil Engineers.

For protection of certain landowners

9. For the protection of the owners the following provisions shall unless otherwise agreed in writing between the Company and the owners apply and have effect:-

(1) In this section, unless the subject or context otherwise requires:-
'the Dol-y-Moch owner' means the owner or owners for the time being of Dol-y-Moch Farm in the urban district of Ffestiniog in the County of Merioneth;
'the Glan-yr-Afon owner' means the owner or owners for the time being of Glan-yr-Afon Farm in the said urban district;
'the owners' means the Dol-y-Moch owner and the Glan-yr-Afon owner;

(2) (a) The Company shall make and maintain for the accommodation of the relevant owner the accommodation works mentioned in column (1) of the following table in the positions denoted on the sealed plan by the letters specified in relation thereto in column (2) of the said table or by agreement with the relevant owner elsewhere within 100 feet on either side of such positions.

(1) Accommodation Works	(2) Position on Sealed Plan
A cattle creep and means of access for persons on foot	A
A level crossing 12 feet in width	B
Culvert to be 4 feet in diameter	C
Culvert to be 4 feet in diameter	D
A level crossing 10 feet in width with graded approaches	E
A crossing 10 feet in width for tractors	F
An overbridge for cattle not less than 4 feet in width	G
A sheep creep 4 feet in width	H
A sheep creep 4 feet in width	J
A level crossing 12 feet in width	K

(3) No station or other facilities for passengers to board or alight from trains shall be constructed or provided on the lands numbered 1 or 2 on the deposited plans.

(4) At least 28 days before the commencement of any calendar year, the Company shall give to the owners notice of the programme of works which they propose to follow in that year for the construction of railway (No. 3) with such documents and information as may be requisite to enable the owners to make representations about such programme of works.

(5) As soon as the Company abandon and discontinue the part of the principal railway situated on the land numbered 2 on the deposited plans they shall give notice thereof to the Dol-y-Moch owner and the Company shall convey, free of charge, the said part of the principal railway (which is shown coloured pink on the sealed plan) and the owner shall accept a conveyance of such land.

Costs of Order

10. All costs, charges and expenses of and incident to the preparing for, obtaining and making of this Order or otherwise in relation thereto shall be paid by the Company and may in whole or in part be defrayed out of revenue.

Given under the Official Seal of the Minister of Transport on 9 February, 1968

C. P. Scott-Malden
An Under Secretary of the
Ministry of Transport

1975 No. 1014
TRANSPORT

Festiniog Railway (Light Railway) (Amendment) Order 1975
Made   17 June, 1975
Coming into Operation   27 June, 1975

The Secretary of State for the Environment on the application of the Festiniog Railway Company and in exercise of powers conferred by sections 7, 9, 10 and 24 of the Light Railways Act 1896 as amended by Light Railways Act 1912 and Part V of the Railways Act 1921 and now vested in him and of all other powers enabling him in that behalf hereby makes the following Order:-

Citation and commencement

1. (1) This Order may be cited as the Festiniog Railway (Light Railway) (Amendment) Order 1975 and shall come into operation on 27 June, 1975.

(2) This Order and the Festiniog Light Railway Orders 1923 and 1968 may be cited together as the Festiniog Light Railway Orders 1923 to 1975.

Power to make railway

4. (1) Subject to the provisions of this Order the Company may make and maintain the railway hereinafter described in the lines and according to the levels and within the limits of deviation shown on the deposited plans and the deposited section and with all proper rails, plates, sidings, junctions, bridges, culverts, drains, approaches, roads, yards, buildings and other works and conveniences connected therewith including station premises at Tan-y-Grisiau.

(2) The said railway is situate wholly in the District of Merionnydd in the County of Gwynedd and is:-

A railway (No. 4) 2,735 metres in length including a tunnel commencing by a junction with the railway (No. 3) at reference point 677428 and terminating by a junction with the principal railway at reference point 683449. (These reference points are National Grid reference points).

Abandonment of part of railway (No. 3)

5. The Company shall not later than the completion and opening for public traffic of railway (No. 4) abandon and discontinue such part of railway (No. 3) as is situate between the commencement of railway (No. 4) and the termination of railway (No. 3).

Power to take lands

6. Subject to the provisions of this Order the Company may enter upon, take and use such of the lands shown on the deposited plans and

described in the deposited book of reference as may be required for the purposes of railway (No. 4).

As to user of railway

7. No part of the railway (No. 4) shall be used for the public conveyance of passengers without the permission in writing of the Secretary of State first being had and obtained which permission shall not be withheld if the Secretary of State is satisfied that such use will not be attended with danger to the public, and the Company shall comply with the conditions (if any) which the Secretary of State may from time to time prescribe for the safety of the public using railway (No. 4).

Power to borrow

8. Notwithstanding anything contained in any previous enactment, the Company may for the purposes of the undertaking and without obtaining any certificate of a justice under section 40 of the Companies Clauses Consolidation Act 1845 borrow, either by way of mortgage of the undertaking or by the creation and issue of debenture stock, or partly by one and partly by the other of those modes, any sum or sums not exceeding in the whole £500,000.

For protection of Central Electricity Generating Board

9. For the protection of the Board the following provisions shall, unless otherwise agreed in writing between the Company and the Board apply and have effect:-

(1) In this section unless the subject or context otherwise requires:-
'the Board' means the Central Electricity Generating Board; 'determined' means agreed in writing between the Company and the Board or in default of agreement determined by arbitration; 'the material section of the railway' means so much of railway (No. 4) as is to be constructed on the protected land and includes that section when so constructed; 'plans' includes sections, specifications and working drawings; 'the protected land' means the land numbered 2 on the deposited plans; 'the signed plans' means the plans comprising sheets Nos 1, 2, 3, 4, 5, and 6 each of which has been signed in duplicate by Leslie John Walshaw Smith on behalf of the Company and by Alick Lowndes Wright on behalf of the Board one copy of which has been deposited with the Company and the other with the Board.

(2) The Company shall not under the powers of this Order acquire compulsorily any lands of the Board but they may acquire, and the Board shall if so required by them, grant to the Company, such easements and rights for a term of years in the lands of the

Board shown on the deposited plans as the Company may reasonably require for the purposes of railway (No. 4).

(3) Notwithstanding anything in section 21 (Power to deviate) of the Order of 1923 as applied to railway (No. 4) by section 3 (Application of parts of Order of 1923) of this Order or shown on the deposited plans the material section of the railway shall not be constructed by the Company except in the line shown on the signed plans.

(4) (a) The Company shall not construct so much of the material section of the railway as lies between reference point 678442 and the northern end of the protected land except in accordance with plans previously submitted to and approved with or without modifications by the Board and subject to such terms and conditions as the Board may think fit to impose;

(b) The said part of the material section of the railway shall be constructed to the satisfaction of the Board and under their supervision.

(5) (a) The Company shall before commencing to construct any other part of the material section of the railway submit to the Board for their reasonable approval plans thereof and of any temporary works to be constructed on the protected land and in giving their approval the Board shall be entitled to take into account the effect on the amenities of the area of the construction of such part of the material section of the railway;

(b) If the Board do not within fifty-six days after the submission to them of any such plans signify to the Company in writing their approval or disapproval thereof they shall be deemed to have approved thereof;

(c) No part of such part of the material section of the railway shall be constructed otherwise than in accordance with such plan as may have been approved (or deemed to have been approved) by the Board or if such approval be withheld as may be settled by arbitration and any such work shall be executed to the reasonable satisfaction of the Board.

(6) (a) The Company shall make and maintain the following works for the accommodation of the Board as the owners of the protected land;

(i) a stockproof gate or cattle grid of such type as may be determined at the southern boundary of the protected land where the railway crosses that boundary from the land numbered 1 on the plans at reference point 677432;

(ii) lockable gates of such type as may be determined where railway (No. 4) crosses the footpath and track between the disused reservoir and the Ystradau measuring weir of the Board at reference point 676434;

(iii) a sheep creep at either of the culverts marked on the plans as culvert No. 3 or culvert No. 4;

(iv) a fence to separate the protected land from railway (No. 4) such fence to be erected on either side of the material section of the railway and of such a type as may be determined.

(b) Where railway (No. 4) crosses any access road of the Board the Company shall comply with the requirements of the Secretary of State and with the reasonable requirements of the Board in respect of train control and safety arrangements;

(c) The works required to be made and maintained by the Company under the foregoing sub-paragraphs shall be treated as being works required by section 68 of the Railways Clauses Consolidation Act 1845 (as incorporated with this Order by section 3 (Application of parts of Order of 1923) of this Order) and the said section 68 shall apply accordingly but nothing in this paragraph shall be taken as prejudicing or affecting the right of the Board under the said section 68 to require the making and maintaining of other works.

(7) The construction of the material section of the railway from reference point 678442 to the northern end of the protected land shall be carried out by a civil engineering contractor to be approved by the Board, and the Company shall complete the construction of that part of the material section of the railway within a period of nine months from the date on which they commence to construct it unless prevented by any cause beyond their control.

(8) (a) The Company shall not during the construction of Railway (No. 4) enter upon and use any existing private road of the Board other than the private access road of the Board from the public road at Dolwen junction to the two points shown on the deposited plans as the points where railway (No. 4) will cross the said private access road on the level

which the Company may enter upon and use subject to such terms and conditions as may be determined;

(b) No vehicles used for or in connection with the construction of railway (No. 4) shall be parked on the said access road.

(9) No explosives shall be used in connection with the making or maintaining of the material section of the railway except at such places and in accordance with such terms and conditions (including conditions relating to the making of excavations in which the explosives are to be placed) as may be approved in writing by the Board.

(10) Where railway (No. 4) crosses the dam of the disused reservoir of the Board on the protected land at reference point 677433 the side cuts in the dam shall be graded to the requirements of the Board and the said disused reservoir shall be fenced by the Company or, if required by the Board filled in.

(11) The Company shall repay to the Board the expenses reasonably incurred by the Board in modifying the Ystradau measuring weir of the Board and required in consequence of the construction of railway (No. 4).

(12) The Company shall instal check rails and barriers of such type as may be determined on the part of railway (No. 4) where it passes the Ffestiniog Generating Station of the Board.

(13) The Board shall permit the Company to use as a storage area the part of the protected land between the site of the former Tan-y-Grisiau Railway Station and Ty'n-y-Pistyll subject to the Company paying compensation if any, to any tenant whose rights may be affected and to reinstating the land to the reasonable satisfaction of the Board on the completion of railway (No. 4).

(14) The Company shall operate the material section of the railway subject to the powers, duties and obligations of the Board in respect of the operation, maintenance and management of their Ffestiniog generating station and associated works.

(15) The Company shall not run trains over the two level crossings referred to in paragraph (8) of this section at a greater frequency than four trains each hour and forty trains each day. Provided that in any peak operating period they may run not more than fifty-two trains over those crossings each day.

(16) (a) If at any time railway (No. 4) or any part thereof has been damaged, abandoned or suffered to fall into a state of disrepair the Company shall, if so required by the Board by notice in writing, either:-

(i) repair or restore railway (No. 4) or any part thereof; or

(ii) remove railway (No. 4) or any part thereof to such extent and in accordance with such conditions as may be reasonably required by the Board.

(b) If on the expiration of 30 days from the date when a notice under sub-paragraph (a) of this paragraph is served upon the Company they have failed to comply with the requirements of the notice the Board may execute the works specified in the notice and recover the reasonable cost thereof (including a proper proportion of the overhead charges of the Board) from the Company.

(17) The Company shall at all times keep the Board indemnified against all damages, losses, costs and expenses which they may sustain or be liable for or reasonably and properly incur by reason or in consequence of any injury, damage or interference which may be caused or may result to any property of the Board in the exercise of any powers conferred by this Order; Provided that the Board shall give to the Company notice of any claim or demand made against them which in the opinion of the Board is a claim or demand for which the Company may be liable under this subsection and no settlement or compromise of any such claim or demand shall be made without the consent in writing of the Company.

(18) If the Stwlan Dam access road of the Board is widened to double carriageway width or is about to be adopted by the highway authority the Company shall provide at their own expense such additional crossing gates or other works (including road improvement works) as will comply with the requirements of the Secretary of State and with the reasonable requirements of the Board or the highway authority.

(19) The fact that any work or thing has been executed or done in accordance with a plan approved or deemed to be approved by the Board or to their satisfaction or in accordance with any directions or award of an arbitrator shall not relieve the Company from any liability under the provisions of this section.

(20) Except as may be otherwise expressly provided by this section any difference arising under this section between the Company and the Board (other than a difference as to the meaning or construction thereof) shall be referred to and determined by an arbitrator to be appointed by agreement between the Company and the Board or, failing agreement on the applica-

tion of either party, after notice in writing to the other by the President of the Institution of Civil Engineers.

Costs of Order

10. All costs, charges and expenses of and incident to the preparing for, obtaining and making of this Order or otherwise in relation thereto shall be paid by the Company and may in whole or in part be defrayed out of revenue.

Signed by authority of
the Secretary of State
17 June, 1975.

W. J. Sharp,
An Under Secretary in the Depart-
partment of the Environment.

Appendix C

FESTINIOG RAILWAY CO
CIVIL ENGINEERING DEPT (NEW WORKS)
LLYN YSTRADAU DEVIATION

INFORMATION SHEET – GENERAL

The nature of the work

The Deviation is being constructed in solid rock and hence the majority of the work is concerned with predrilling the rock for blasting and then transporting the debris to the embankments. Most of the effort is concentrated on loading rock into skips, for this is the job which basically determines the speed with which the project progresses.

The principles by which the Deviation is being built are the same as was used by the Victorian railway builders, except that where they drilled their shot holes using a heavy hammer on the drill steels, we use power tools. The cuttings are dug full face immediately to their final depth and the spoil is transported to the adjacent embankment. To facilitate this, temporary track in prefabricated sections is laid on the newly built formation, on which skips run carrying the shattered rock.

Where the line crosses streams, culverts are built and at strategic points underpasses for the benefit of sheep. Sometimes on particularly precipitous ground dry stone retaining walls are constructed to reduce the amount of spoil to be moved. At other points there are bridges to be built and a tunnel as well. All these activities represent work for volunteers.

Joining a working party

If you feel you would like to work on the Deviation and wish to ensure that your efforts are utilised to the best advantage, then you should join one of the established groups or working parties. The nature of the work generally means that volunteers work in gangs of three or four people and it is a great advantage when a gang, once formed, can be kept together for as long as possible. The lone volunteer who turns up out of the blue with half a day to spare may be lucky and immediately find himself in a job he can do, but it may well be that at that moment there is nobody available to explain to him what to do and how to do it.

Weekend working parties are run throughout the year in accordance with an annually published fixture list, which allots alternate weekends to London group and the intermediate weekends to parties from Manchester and Gloucester areas. Application to join one of these parties can be made to the appropriate organiser by telephone about a week in advance or alternatively by letter, enclosing an S.A.E. in which case about ten days notice is required. Each group makes their own arrangements about transport which is generally in private cars. Your area group organiser will be able to give you more information.

During the period of university vacations there is a fairly steady stream of groups working on the Deviation. Some of these groups are run for the benefit of members of a particular organisation, but there are also groups which are built up from applications to work from individual volunteers. Details of the planned weekday working parties can be obtained from the weekday working party organiser, whose address appears on the fixture list.

Any volunteer who is prepared to give what he can towards the construction of the Deviation will find a welcome at Dduallt.

Working party supervision

Due to the nature of the work and the fact that there is only one person permanently employed by the railway company to supervise work on the Deviation, it is necessary that all working parties exceeding five in number must provide their own supervisors. For this purpose a supervisor is considered to be a person who is au fait with the current state of Deviation work and who is capable of controlling the activities of five or six other volunteers, ensuring that they know what to do and work in a safe and sensible manner. This particularly applies to organisers of weekday working parties who have reserved one of the Messes for their sole use, since otherwise it is the responsibility of the regular organisers to see that this condition is met.

Accommodation

Volunteers, whilst working on the Deviation, can be accommodated in either Dduallt Mess (12 beds) or Moelwyn Tunnel Mess (24 beds). The decision as to which Mess is to be used rests with the appropriate group organiser as detailed on the fixture list or the resident Site Agent.

Maps

The maps covering the area are the One Inch Ordnance Survey series sheets number 107 (Dolgelley) and 116 (Snowdon).

Access

The site of current Deviation work and both Messes can only be approached by rail or on foot. During that part of the year when a regular public train service is operating the easiest means of access to Dduallt for a person unfamiliar with the territory is by train from the Festiniog Railway Co's Tan-y-Bwlch Station on the Maentwrog – Rhyd – Llanfrothen road. Car parking facilities are available at this station, but in view of the restricted space available it is much appreciated if cars are parked such as to occupy the minimum area. If in doubt as to the best place for long term parking consult the parking attendant or the station master. Rail passengers should alight at Campbells Platform (Request Halt) for Dduallt Mess (O.S. Grid Ref: 67354180), or Dduallt Station for the site of Deviation work and the Moelwyn Tunnel Mess (O.S. Grid Ref: 68004275).

Access on foot is possible by the path leading from Bron Turner (O.S. Grid Ref: 66704130) to Dduallt Station, passing Dduallt Mess and crossing the railway line on the way. Cars can be parked on the grass to the left of the track leading up to Bron Turner cottage after crossing the ford. This is possible by kind permission of the landowner and every effort should be made to cause no offence or inconvenience by inconsiderate parking or leaving of litter. The ford, which has a gravel bottom, can after periods of prolonged and heavy rain, become impassable.

Outside of peak train operating periods Deviationists can push their luggage up the line from Tan-y-Bwlch to Dduallt on one of the purpose built trolleys. This however is only permissible under the supervision of an officially recognised trolley operator, who must have obtained beforehand train staff clearance for the section. The return journey is made under the influence of gravity.

There is also a footpath from Tan-y-Grisiau to Dduallt along the west side of Llyn Ystradau (known as Tan-y-Grisiau Reservoir in CEGB parlance), which is marked on electricity board land by a series of white posts. It is of use to those coming from Blaenau

175

Ffestiniog on foot, but is not recommended for walking after dark for those unfamiliar with its route. After passing round the lake the path leads over the top of the old Moelwyn Incline and down past the Moelwyn Tunnel Mess running roughly parallel to the route of the railway until it reaches Dduallt Station.

Dduallt Mess

Dduallt Mess is a converted barn attached to a very ancient and historic house owned and occupied by Col and Mrs A. Campbell. It is situated some fifty feet below the railway at the request halt called naturally enough Campbells Platform. Converted between October 1964 when the project started and October 1965, this Mess has beds for approximately fourteen people. The facilities provided here include hot and cold running water, toilet, shower, washbasins, electric lighting, cooking facilities and an open log fire.

The Mess is divided into basically two main rooms, one of which contains a series of two-tier bunks and the other the living and cooking areas. Washing facilities are housed in separate cubicles, whilst the toilet is now placed in a recently converted annexe, which ultimately will also house further sleeping accommodation.

Timber for the fire is normally stacked either at Campbells Platform or immediately outside the Mess. The fuel is mostly logs from trees cut down in building the railway, very old railway sleepers, or fence posts. A small quantity of wood is kept inside the Mess drying in preparation for lighting the next fire. All departing groups should ensure that this is done for the benefit of the following group. Experience has shown that the fire is best started using paper and small twigs, gradually increasing the size of the wood as the fire gets going until finally the larger logs are added. The fire rarely, if ever, needs to be lit during the summer months.

The switch for the immersion heater is to be found in the cupboard with the blue door next to the shower. A pilot light glows above the main entrance when it is on. Care must be taken by departing groups to ensure that the heater is switched off at the end of their stay.

Rubbish should be deposited on the tip which Mrs Campbell will be pleased to point out to any enquirer, and immediately burnt so as to avoid the development of offensive smells. It is also important that rubbish should not be allowed to accumulate in the Mess since this encourages the breeding of mice.

The water supply for the Mess comes from a tank higher up the hillside, which is fed by a mountain stream. This supply can be treated like a normal domestic system, but in periods of extremely severe frost it has been known to freeze up. The main stopcock for the supply is to be found on the floor of the washroom at the lower end of the Mess.

Moelwyn Tunnel Mess

The Moelwyn Tunnel Mess is a sectional timber building some 60ft by 20ft fully lined internally and providing beds for twenty-four people. It is situated about a quarter mile north of Dduallt Station at the mouth of the now abandoned Moelwyn Tunnel. It is best approached by walking along the old railway line from the station, but a watch must be kept for vehicles on the line since it is in use for construction purposes.

The facilities provided include hot and cold running water, though the hot supply is somewhat temperamental, toilets, showers, wash-basins, Calor gas lighting, cooking facilities and a super efficient coke stove. The Mess is divided up into three sections, with a sleeping area at either end containing three-tier bunks and a large living space in the middle. Toilets and washing facilities are housed in separate cubicles.

The water supply is derived from a dam built inside the old tunnel from which it flows to a low level tank just outside the Mess. A hand pump is provided to lift the water up to a high level tank, which then feeds the Mess. During the winter period (Nov to March incl) the entire water system must be drained to avoid frost damage when the Mess is not occupied. The pump must be disconnected and all the taps in the Mess left open.

The hotwater is heated by a Calor gas unit very similar in style to a domestic 'Ascot'. Before it will work the pilot light must be lit and it can then be left on for however long the Mess is occupied. Detailed instructions for operation and draining are written on the unit.

Rubbish from the Mess should be deposited at the foot of an embankment under construction, burnt and then covered with stones. The cinders from the stove should be spread on the path around the side of the Mess. No refuse whatsoever is to be dumped on land not belonging to the Festiniog Railway Company.

The Calor gas cylinders are kept in a special housing outside the Mess at its southern end. Two cylinders can be connected up at any one time but only one is on tap. The changeover valve, which registers when the cylinder is empty, enables the cylinder in use to be changed without switching off all the appliances. Empty cylinders should be removed immediately. The cylinders should be turned off when the Mess is unoccupied.

The two toilets in this Mess are of the Perdisan drain-connected chemical variety. Instructions for operating and maintaining these units in good order are posted in each toilet and it is essential for trouble-free service that the instructions are carefully followed.

Mess charges and accounts

The standard charge for food and accommodation at either Mess is 10/- (50p) per day. This charge covers the operating costs only since the use of the buildings is provided free by the railway company.

The accounts are kept in a special book which must be completed by each group accurately listing all the sources of income and expenditure. The totals must be brought forward and the difference tallied with the cash in hand. All bills must be paid and any surplus banknotes accumulating should be changed into a cheque payable to the 'Bradshaw and Schumann Acct'. The cheque should then either be sent to the Mess Secretary, in which case the amount should then be entered in the expenditure column as 'Transferred to B. & S. Acct.' or alternatively just left in the cash box.

Food supplies

Delivery of food

All foodstuffs are normally delivered to Tan-y-Bwlch Station by the suppliers. Providing John Harrison, the stationmaster, is advised beforehand he will ensure that arriving provisions are placed under cover, if no Deviationist is on hand to receive them. During the summer season, when passenger trains are operating, the group organiser should, when feasible, arrange that somebody is detailed to be at Tan-y-Bwlch Station to receive incoming supplies and to help load them on to the train if required. Due to the restricted space available in the guards van, very large deliveries may necessitate the attaching of a special van to the train, in which case the stationmaster should be consulted beforehand.

Food specific

It should be noted that tinned peaches and pineapple are over twice as expensive as rhubarb and gooseberries and therefore over a period of time the consumption of each should be balanced. One large-sized tin of fruit (A10) should feed at least fifteen people.

Out of season fruit and vegetables at inflated prices should not be purchased.

Potatoes should be purchased in units of 56lbs (25kg) and sugar in packs of 14 No 2lbs (ie 28lbs or metric equivalent).

Non-perishable foodstuffs

The following is a list of provisions that are normally purchased in bulk by the Mess Secretary and should not normally be purchased by individual groups unless stocks have completely run out and no suitable alternative is available.

Peaches	Dried Milk
Pineapples	Condensed Milk
Victoria Plums	Orange Squash
Pears	Lemon Squash
Rhubarb	Coffee
Gooseberries	Porridge Oats
Tomatoes	Sugar
Peas	Jams, various
Carrots (tinned)	Golden syrup
Branston pickle	Stewing Steak
Salad Cream	Soups, various
Cooking Oil	Baked Beans
Condiments	

Toilet Rolls	Soap
Toilet Chemicals	Detergents

Typical Menu

This menu is intended as a guide to help those ordering food to keep within the limit of the funds available.

Breakfast   Porridge
Bacon or sausages and egg
Bread, butter and jams
Tea or coffee

Lunch   Bread, butter, cheese, jams, pickles
Cake and biscuits
Fruit
Squash
Soup (winter only)

Supper   Soup
Steak and kidney stew containing onions, carrots, tomatoes
Cabbage
Potatoes
Tinned fruit and condensed milk
Tea or coffee

Consumption rates

Based on the above menu the following consumption rates per man day have from experience been found to be adequate and to be within the limits set by the Mess charge. These should be ordered well in advance from the specified supplier:-

Eggs	one
Bacon	$\frac{1}{8}$lb (60gm)
or Sausages	$\frac{1}{4}$lb (115gm)
Milk	$\frac{1}{2}$ pint ($\frac{1}{4}$ litre)
Bread, large	$\frac{1}{3}$ loaf
Cheese	$\frac{1}{10}$lb (45gm)
Onions	$\frac{1}{10}$lb (45gm)
Carrots	$\frac{1}{5}$lb (90gm)
Steak and kidney	$\frac{2}{5}$lb (180gm)
Cabbage	$\frac{1}{10}$th
Apple or orange	one
Butter	$\frac{1}{5}$lb (90gm)

Menus

For the benefit of groups staying at Dduallt for some time the Mess Secretary will prepare, on request, a suggested menu tailored to the cooking skills of the group.

Calor gas

The gas cylinders are delivered by the supplier, Eric Owen Ltd, of 117 High Street, PORTHMADOG, (Tel Porthmadog 2525), to Tan-y-Bwlch Station, although during the summer period they sometimes come all the way up to Dduallt on the train from Porthmadog. Similarly empty cylinders should be left at Tan-y-Bwlch or placed on a Porthmadog bound train with a label attached reading, 'Return empty to Eric Owen Ltd, from Dduallt'.

Dduallt Mess uses the small 33lb grey cylinders (butane gas), whilst the Moelwyn Tunnel Mess uses the 104lb red cylinders (propane gas). It is not possible accidentally to use the wrong gas since the cylinders are fitted with different types of connections.

When the Messes are left unoccupied the gas cylinders should be turned off. When supplies of gas run low the Mess Secretary should be informed so that new cylinders can be ordered. In the event of the supply actually running out a full cylinder can be obtained direct from Eric Owen Ltd, in exchange for an empty one. If this is done the Mess Secretary should be informed of the fact and given up to date details of the cylinder stock position. It is most important that cylinders are returned to the supplier immediately they are empty.

Beer supply

The Moelwyn Tunnel Mess has a CO_2 powered beer supply permanently on tap, but the supply in Dduallt Mess is generally only available at periods of peak demand. The charge for beer is 2/6d (12p) per pint.

When supplies of beer run low the Mess Secretary, whose address and telephone number appear on the 'Fixture List', should be contacted to arrange for a new barrel to be delivered. It is obtained from the Church Place Wine Stores (proprietor Mrs Edwards), PENRHYNDEUDRAETH, Merioneth (Tel Penrhyndeudraeth 533).

Fresh barrels are normally delivered to Tan-y-Bwlch Station and empty barrels should be left there for collection. When the train service is running the barrels are often brought up to Dduallt on the train.

First aid

First aid kits are provided in both Messes and in the tool shed at Dduallt Station. Each kit contains the normal supply of Elastoplast, bandages and disinfectant.

In cases of injury or suspected infected cuts, which are beyond the resources of the first aid kits, the injured person should be taken to the casualty department of the hospital at Porthmadog.

In cases of emergency, when a doctor or ambulance is needed, ring Porthmadog Station as they have a GPO telephone and can make the necessary arrangements. Alternatively Col Campbell has a GPO phone at Dduallt Mess.

Telephones

All stations and principal buildings on the railway are connected to the company's own automatic telephone system. This network is entirely separate from the GPO and through calls between the two systems cannot be made. The telephones operate in exactly the same way as normal dial instruments except that a pause must be left between each set of digits. A complete list of dialling codes is displayed adjacent to each phone.

Security

Despite the remoteness of the sites, experience has shown that vandalism and theft are events against which precautions must be taken. It is therefore prudent to lock all buildings when left unattended for any length of time, and to chain all the skips to the track, preferably in a cutting, when the sites are not being worked. Valuable items, if they must be left in the Messes, should be hidden away out of sight.

Public footpaths, etc

It is most desirable that good relations should be maintained with the surrounding landowners. Volunteers are therefore expected to keep to the local footpaths, which are marked on the relevant ordnance survey maps, and to the property of the Festiniog Railway Co.

Walking along the railway track between Tan-y-Bwlch and Dduallt Stations can be highly dangerous due to the restricted clearance between trains and earthworks, and should not be attempted during train operating periods. At all other times a sharp lookout should be maintained for unscheduled trains. It should be pointed out that trains in the downhill direction make almost no noise at all and only a visual lookout will give warning of their coming.

There is a footpath available between Dduallt Station and Dduallt Mess, which continues on down to the Vale of Ffestiniog to come out on to the valley road near the Oakley Arms Hotel at Bron Turner. (See – Access.) This footpath should be used at all times in preference to walking along the railway track. Where it is absolutely necessary to walk on the track, care should be taken to walk only down the centre of the track so as to avoid pushing the ballast into the ditches.

Free travel facilities

Persons working on the Deviation are granted by the Festiniog Railway Co, the right to travel free at their own risk on public passenger trains operated by the Company. However if the train is full, the guard may refuse permission to ride depending on the degree of importance of the proposed journey. During the peak holiday period, trains, particularly in the middle of the day, tend to be full.

Digging techniques

The basic hand tools for digging on the Deviation are:-
(a) The pick-mattock which is similar to the well-known pickaxe except that one of the points is replaced by a blade about three inches wide. The point is used for loosening material, whilst the blade is used for dragging material down the cutting face and breaking up relatively soft ground. The blade can also be used as

a chisel to break up blocks of stratified rock and also, if inserted in a crack in the rock and twisted, to loosen rocks in the cutting face.

(b) Crowbars, which are available in various sizes, are used to dislodge rocks held fairly firmly in the cutting face.

(c) Spalling hammers, weighing about 10lbs, are provided for breaking up boulders which are too large to manhandle into the skips. When being used on hard rock there is a danger from flying splinters, and those in the vicinity are strongly advised to take precautions to protect their eyes.

(d) Two types of shovels are in use. The square-ended ones are most effective when shovelling off a flat surface. The pointed ones, known either as klondike or heart-shaped shovels, are very useful when digging in stony material on a rough surface.

The digging crew for a cutting face is normally four people filling one skip. If more are employed they tend to get in each other's way. Two people bring the rock down to the cutting floor, whilst the other two shovel it into the skip. The full skips are run to the end of the embankment for tipping along temporary track. It is good practice to arrange for the last length of track before the tip end to run uphill for not only does it assist in stopping the full wagons, but also allows for the subsidence that inevitably occurs amongst the freshly-tipped rock. Should the stage be reached where the track droops down at the tip end then the incidence of skips lost over the end will increase. It is much easier to trim an embankment down to level than to make it up. Where the embankments are being constructed out of stratified rock, the end-tipping wagons should be used in preference, and the embankments constructed to their full 10ft width immediately. The side-tipping skips are used principally for conveying topsoil for tipping on the sides of the finished embankments.

Experience has shown that the loose and shattered rock in a cutting can most easily be dug out when there is a flat surface underneath from which to shovel. The most efficient way of digging out the spoil has therefore been found to be when the advancing cutting face is kept as steep as possible and boards of wood or steel are placed on the ground at track formation level up to the foot of the face. The rock face can then easily be collapsed on to the boards and shovelled away off the flat surface. As soon as it is possible to dig out in advance of the shovelling boards, they should be advanced forward to the face again. It is most important that the boards are not allowed to rise above the finished formation level. Also, the temptation to landslide the face down on to the boards without digging out the bottom of the cutting and bringing them forward, must be resisted. Where a hard block of rock is encountered in the cutting floor, as from time to time occurs, this must be removed by use of the air breaker, or blasting, as soon as possible. A cutting which is being managed well, will have a floor of uniform gradient and width, with a steep advancing face, at the foot of which will be a neat array of shovelling boards. In advance of the face the overburden will have been stripped off preparatory to the next round of drilling and blasting.

Once the very loose rock created by blasting has been removed, the remaining rock will be found to have been shattered into blocks, but left still in its original position. It is then that the skill of the digger becomes important, for there is no point in rushing madly at the face with pick and crowbar, and trying to extract the nearest piece of rock to hand. The face must be scientifically dismantled, starting with those rock layers that are nearest the ground surface. Where the rock grain slopes across the width of the cutting, there is sometimes an advantage to be gained from advancing one side of the face ahead of the other.

It is not possible to give adequate instructions on shot hole patterns since this is largely a matter of personal experience, but the most important point to be watched is that all shot holes drilled down to the full cutting depth, should be extended at least one foot below formation level.

Appendix D
The Deviation in Verse
and Song

The Deviation, alas, had no muse – as readers will no doubt agree
from the verses which follow. It did, however, have a Bard, as those
who have ever roared out Chris Chitty's rousing choruses will
certainly affirm. Beginning with such verses as there are, we find
David Yates of Northern Group writing to David Currant at
Observatory Gardens, London, on 24 August, 1968:

> T' ye all,
>
> T' Northern Group I write t' say
> 'as t' work on t' Saturday
> In t' wilds o' Wales we'r sent
> T' dig a railway be' bent
>
> As we lift 'r glass o'ale
> And spin an other railway tale
> We'll think o' Junta and o' thee
> Down south in t' Observatory
>
> Wit' double blast o' o'd Fairlie
> Or t' beat o' Prince or t' Lady
> We join t'gether wi' one ambition
> T' Llyn Ystradau Deviation

from the *Moelwyn Express and Dduallt Daily Digger* No 6, 1971
> We are the lumberjacks and we're O.K.
> We sleep all night and we work all day,
> Nick is a narcoleptic so they say
> He sleeps all night and he sleeps all day

THE WAR SONG OF DINAS FAWR

The mountain sides are steeper
But the valley floors are flatter;
We therefore deemed it neater
To lay rails in the latter.
Our ancient foeman seized this vale:
Our bed and track denied us –
He stole our rail from Hill and dale
And eighteen years defied us.

But see how sweet revenge is still,
And faceless men o'erthrowing,
By cut and fill we climbed this hill,
Our rails to Blaenau going;
And if we meet that foe again,
That law for justice barters,
We'll drive a train straight through his brain,
And have his guts for garters.

So now we stand on new-won land,
Between the lakes electric;
And drive again the faceless men
To aspect apoplectic:
So CEGB, the king of MANWEB fled,
His floods we drove before us:
His poles and wires shall feed our fires,
His overthrow, our chorus.
With apologies to Thomas Love Peacock (1785-1866)
Devised by Peter Jarvis

DEVIATION SONGS

NO BRAKE ON MY TROLLEY
by Chris Chitty

No brake on my trolley, so we're just rollin' along,
We're coming down without a staff,
Train is due, what a laugh
And we're singing a happy song, Oh yeah!

Singing cuttings and ditches go thundering by
But me and my trolley will never say die,
In just half a mile there's Campbell's siding
And we can watch old Garraway go steaming by.

No brake on my trolley, so we're just rollin' along
We don't really care one bit, the train is near
We're just in it
But we're singing a happy song, Oh yeah!

Singing cuttings and ditches go thundering by,
But me and my trolley will never say die,
Just round the bend there's Campbell's siding
And we can watch old Garraway go steaming by.

No brake on our trolley, so we're just rollin' along
The train is getting very near,
Oh my gawd! it's *Mountaineer*,
But we're singing a happy song, Oh yeah!

Singing cuttings and ditches go thundering by
But me and my trolley will never say die,
In just twenty yards there's Campbell's siding,
And we can watch old Garraway go steaming by.

No brake on our trolley, so we hit *Mountaineer*,
Made poor Alan scream and swear,
Dancing there and pulling out his hair,
But we're singing a happy song. Oh yeah!

Singing, Oh my gawd lads, we're in a hell of a jam,
But we can always join the Towyn Tram
And one fine day before we die we'll return
To watch old Garraway go steaming by.

(Chris Chitty writes in connection with this song . . . 'in the early years of the Deviation around 1969 we were not held in high esteem by the rest of the railway. There were many, the General Manager included, who thought we were wasting our time. This situation was made worse when Gerald Fox gravitated down the line towards Minffordd to meet a train coming up. Our only mode of transport in those days was by trolley to T-y-B and these facts are what gave rise to this song. Alan Garraway drove *Mountaineer* for a short while to relieve Roy Goldstraw, whose daughter Helen (a notable Deviationist) was in hospital in Llandudno following a motor bike accident.')

THE RUNAWAY SKIP
by Chris Chitty and Douglas Dick
T'was in the summer of '69
On that old Festiniog line,
And work on Barn Site was so very slow
The rocks were wet, the rails were cold,
And Bunny's boot just would not hold,
And so a skip went rolling down the hill.

Oh! the runaway skip went down the track and it flew
You should see the old skip rock and sway
The mad axeman's taken the line away
And it flew.

T'was in the summer of '69
On that old Festiniog line,

The coal was bad, the fire was poor
And so the fire just would not draw,
The brakes began to leak on more and more.

Oh! *Mountaineer* came slowly down the hill,
You should hear old Goldstraw curse like ten,
His engine's stuck in the tunnel again,
For a blow.

T'was in the summer of '69,
On that old Festiniog line,
And work on Dragon had come to a stop
We drilled some holes into the rock,
The Colonel filled them to the top,
And said, 'we're going to have a great big bang'.

Oh! Colonel Campbell lit the fuse and ran,
You should hear the farmer curse and swear,
As great big rocks fell everywhere,
On his land.

T'was in the summer of '69,
On that old Festiniog line,
And work on Dingle site was rather slack,
The whistle announced the train had come
For the buffet car the diggers ran,
The Northern Group came pounding down the track.

Oh! The Northern Group ran for the train
And the buffet car ran dry again,
And they blew.

(The 'Mad Axeman' was a frequent volunteer on the Deviation;
he was devoid of personality, and was a menace on site, hence his
name. The last verse was written by Douglas Dick who made such
a habit of meeting the train for a swift one that the Company had to
put a ban on it.)

Chris Chitty wrote most of his songs for the Sunday evening 'Beer
Train', always a high spot in the social calendar of the Deviationists.
It made very little in fares but plenty in profits on drink, since pubs in
this part of Wales do not open on Sundays.

Index